Let's Go Outside!

Related High/Scope Press Preschool Publications

Educating Young Children: Active Learning Practices for Preschool and Child Care Programs

A Study Guide to Educating Young Children: Exercises for Adult Learners

Extensions—Newsletter of the High/Scope Curriculum

The Teacher's Idea Book 1: Planning Around the Key Experiences

The Teacher's Idea Book 2: Planning Around Children's Interests

The Teacher's Idea Book 3: 100 Small-Group Experiences

Supporting Young Learners 1: Ideas for Preschool and Day Care Providers

Supporting Young Learners 2: Ideas for Child Care Providers and Teachers

Getting Started: Materials and Equipment for Active Learning Preschools

*Movement Plus Rhymes, Songs, & Singing Games, Second Edition,
and accompanying music recordings* (cassette, CD)

How Adults Support Children at Planning Time (video)

How Adults Support Children at Work Time (video)

How Adults Support Children at Recall Time (video)

Supporting Children in Resolving Conflicts (video)

Adult-Child Interactions: Forming Partnerships With Children (video)

High/Scope Child Observation Record (COR) for Ages 2½– 6

High/Scope COR-PC and COR-Mac for Ages 2½– 6

High/Scope Program Quality Assessment (PQA)

Available from

High/Scope® Press
A division of the
High/Scope Educational Research Foundation
600 North River Street, Ypsilanti, MI 48198-2898
ORDERS: phone (800)40-PRESS, fax (800)442-4FAX
e-mail: press@highscope.org
www.highscope.org

Let's Go Outside!
Designing the Early Childhood Playground

Tracy Theemes

HIGH/SCOPE PRESS

Ypsilanti, Michigan

Published by
HIGH/SCOPE® PRESS

A division of the High/Scope Educational Research Foundation
600 North River Street
Ypsilanti, Michigan 48198-2898
(734)485-2000, fax (734)485-0704
press@highscope.org, www.highscope.org

Holly Barton, *High/Scope Press Editor*
Margaret FitzGerald, *Metaphor Marketing Inc., Cover design, text design, and production*
Photographs on pp. 11, 44 (bottom), 45, 49, and 57 by Mogens Tom Jensen, Denmark
All other photos by Gregory Fox Photography, Ann Arbor, Michigan

Library of Congress Cataloging-in-Publication Data

Theemes, Tracy, 1960-
      Let's go outside! : designing the early childhood playground / by
Tracy Theemes.
           p.   cm.
      Includes bibliographical references (p.) and index.
      ISBN 1-57379-082-6
      1. Playgrounds--Design and construction. 2. Playgrounds-
-Equipment and supplies--Design and construction. 3. Play.
4. Early childhood education. I. Title.
GV425.T54   1999
711'.558--dc21   99-34787
                                                                              CIP

Printed in the United States of America
10 9 8 7 6 5 4 3 2 1

Contents

Preface

I watch as Michael moves from one corner of the playground to another. In each corner, he bends down to begin his daily digging. Scooping out handfuls of sand at each location, he carefully buries a block or a small plastic animal he has stored in his pocket. Then he replaces the sand and pats it down until it is smooth. Today he only takes a few minutes to complete his work before running off to find his friend Sam. Together, Sam and Michael begin to chase Chin. The three boys come across a soccer ball, and their chasing evolves into a spontaneous game of soccer.

Rachel, who has almost mastered the challenge of climbing the overhead ladder, is diligent about her daily sessions. First she climbs one rung and drops to the ground. Brushing the sand off her tights, she looks up, appearing to reassess the situation. This time she climbs three rungs, and a look of triumph flashes across her face.

Behind the playhouse, I observe Benjamin as he sits on a swing, watching the others. It's difficult to tell from his expression if he is sad or just thoughtful.

Play is the medium of children's expression, whether a child is coming to grips with the death and funeral of a baby brother, like Michael, or is simply expressing the exuberance of youth. The importance of play in the life of a child cannot be ignored. Landreth (1993) states that "for children to play out their experiences and feelings is the most natural, dynamic, and self-healing process in which children can engage. It is a process in which they can build up their confidence in dealing with their environment" (p. 17). Rogers and Sharapan (1993) concur that "play is an expression of our creativity. It is at the very root of our ability to learn, to cope, and to become whatever we may be" (p. 5). Wasserman (1992) states that "play allows children to make discoveries that go far beyond the realm of what we adults think is important to know . . . with play, we teachers can have it all: the development of knowledge, of a spirit of inquiry, of creativity, of conceptual understanding—all contributing to the true empowerment of children" (p. 133).

Outdoor play is commonly believed to be an important form of play for young children. Teachers include it in their daily plans, parents admonish their children to "get some fresh air," and the press decries the replacement of traditional outdoor play with passive entertainment. Although there is little controversy about the necessity of outside play, there is some confusion about what children and adults should actually do outside.

This book has been written to help teachers and caregivers of children through age 8 establish safe yet effective outdoor play spaces where children can engage freely in active learning experiences. To make full use of the play space as a resource for learning, we will consider several key questions: What do children gain from outdoor play? How can we as teachers keep children safe, yet allow them to challenge themselves? What is our role on the playground? In addition, we will look at the key elements of playground design, examine the way the developmental characteristics of young children influence playground design, and offer a framework for furnishing and maintaining the outdoor classroom.

Play is a powerful medium for children's growth and development, and the outdoor play space can be used to promote exploration, physical activity, and positive social interactions. The arrangement of the outdoor space—the pattern of movement and the balance of equipment—can greatly influence the success of the playground. Creating the best playground for your particular space and program is challenging, but the rewards to children are well worth it.

Let's Go Outside!

1 Why Playgrounds?

Play as a Medium for Learning

Although play is sometimes regarded as frivolous by adults, the idea that "play is children's work" is readily accepted by professionals working with young children. This suggests that there are myriad ways to learn. For example, an adult might learn to fix a carburetor by reading a manual, to tie flies for fishing by watching a video, or to use algorithms by listening to a lecture. Young children, however, learn best by playing because they can actively and naturally explore, discover, experiment, and practice their new skills. In supporting children's natural desire to play, adults encourage them to discover things for themselves and to continue to build their knowledge base. As their knowledge increases, children's play becomes more complex.

> Playing is learning, and outdoor play opens up a vast array of learning experiences.
>
> **HARRIS, 1996, p. 122**

The Elements of Outdoor Play

Play includes the following basic elements:

1. **Play is pleasurable and gratifying.** A child will continue to play as long as possible and, if interrupted, will try to resume the activity. Play might possess elements of daring or mystery, but the overriding experience will be one of enjoyment.

2. **Play is self-directed and engaged in freely.** If an adult imposes a goal or set of rules that the child did not establish or agree to independently, the spontaneous enjoyment of the play is lost and the child may quickly lose interest in it.

3. **Play is intrinsically rewarding for children.** The *process* of play is what makes it meaningful to young children. The presence of an external reward can rob children of the joy of doing something just because they want to.
4. **Play is challenging, active, and engaging.** A play activity must be interesting enough to hold attention but not so challenging as to cause frustration or stress. Play is most beneficial when the skill of the player and the level of challenge are closely matched.
5. **Play is imaginative.** Everyday objects take on many new and exciting meanings. What is just a patch of grass to an adult can become a swamp filled with alligators to a child at play.

The Value of Outdoor Play

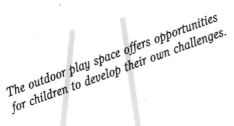
The outdoor play space offers opportunities for children to develop their own challenges.

When children go out to play, they want to feel a sense of mystery and adventure. They also need to feel a sense of security, of being well cared for and protected. They want a place where they can be with other children, or daydream in quiet solitude. They want to be able to test themselves, find their limits, and push past them because "in play, children expand the borders of their lives" (Alberta Parks and Recreation, 1987, p. 4).

Outdoor play can foster children's development in several areas. Primary benefits of playing outdoors include

- Contact with nature
- Opportunities for social play
- Freedom of movement and active physical play

Contact With Nature

The absence of a roof and walls allows children to explore a larger world—to investigate nature and form their own ideas and observations. Discoveries await as children and adults observe birds building a nest, watch ants scurry across the sidewalk, and explore the rough bark of a tree. Children also have a chance to discover for themselves such principles as "what goes up must come down" as they throw a ball into the air.

Heat, cold, rain, snow, sun, and wind all change the outdoor scene and offer children different and exciting opportunities for exploration. Experiencing nature's wonderful "mess" can help children develop an appreciation and respect for the natural world. As the seasons change, many children experience the thrill of falling leaves, swirling snow, and blooming flowers. Not only are these experiences rich in themselves but they also help broaden children's understanding of nature's changes over time.

Opportunities for Social Play

The social play that takes place inside the preschool or child care setting continues out on the playground. Children look for a friend with whom to share a discovery, make observations, and establish roles in a play scene. Initiative, cooperation, turn taking, and conflict resolution are a few of the important social skills that are learned indoors but can be further developed on the playground.

Nature is full of rich discoveries for both children and adults.

Freedom of Movement and Active Physical Play

Outdoor play usually offers greater freedom of movement and more physical challenges than indoor environments can accommodate. The louder and more active environment allows for different types of child-child and child-

By playing with peers, children gain experience in leading, following, cooperating—and problem solving!

environment interaction than is possible indoors. Many children (and adults!) have become more sedentary than in the past; by encouraging outdoor play, we enable children to indulge their innate enjoyment of movement in a natural setting and to develop healthy, lifelong habits.

Safety Versus Challenge

Children's play becomes a learning experience when it includes both enjoyment and appropriate challenges. Practicing newly emerging skills is an instinctive drive in young children—as evidenced by the toddler who falls countless times while learning to walk but gets right back up each time. Adults need to support children as they experiment with their bodies and practice important physical skills. Thus, a basic challenge for play-space designers is to provide an outdoor environment that enables children to take risks and stretch their capabilities and yet protects them from harming themselves or others. It is not always easy to balance children's needs for physical and mental challenges with the adults' needs to protect children—often from those same challenges!

Trying out new skills is an exciting part of outdoor play for children.

What are the consequences of solving this dilemma by making playgrounds safe without regard to children's need for challenge? Much of today's popular playground equipment contains safe design elements—low heights, accommodations for only one child at a time, and single-purpose use—that can quickly become predictable for children. If play equipment and outdoor activities are not challenging or varied enough or do not give children an opportunity to use their imaginations and satisfy their curiosity, children may become bored and start to engage in risky behavior outdoors. You may see children standing on fences, diving off the tops of swings or slides, or using materials such as branches and rope dangerously.

Under-challenging playgrounds may also result in some children, particularly those of elementary age, satisfying their need for challenge and adventure in places where there is no adult supervision or guidance. For example, when observing a small-town playground with an active risk-management program, I witnessed a group of 7–9-year-old boys challenging each other to get up on a swing set to leap off the crossbeam. This was only a few days after I observed similar kinds of behavior with 10–11-year-old girls doing back flips off the storage hut, in the same standard-compliant playground. Heseltine (1995, p. 91) summarizes why we must make playgrounds as challenging to young children as the indoor learning environment:

Children are able to express themselves freely outdoors!

> We have forgotten why we have playgrounds.
> They are for children to play on. . . . We have
> forgotten the essentially exploratory and investigatory nature
> of play, of what the process is about—of challenging and
> developing mind and body. We have made playgrounds so safe
> that children are forced to find their way round the safety
> measure solely to be able to enjoy themselves and to play—
> and have accidents as a result.

Yet, providing the challenges children need to play in a productive manner does not negate the need to provide also for their safety and security. Emotional safety is as important as physical safety in children's outdoor activities, and it is the obligation of the adults who work with young children to ensure that the level of risk involved in outdoor play is appropriate to the age of the children and that there are no hidden dangers in playground structures that could harm them. Throughout this book I will offer guidelines for balancing safety and challenge in ways that neither compromise the well-being of children nor limit their opportunities for adventure and excitement.

The first playgrounds appeared in Europe in the 1800's as open spaces where children had freely played were gradually replaced by urban housing complexes.

Whether the focus is on health, gross-motor skills, social competence, fun, or discovery, the underlying purpose of the outdoor playground is to promote children's development in a safe, secure environment.

Summary

Playgrounds allow children to move in a freer, more active way, to interact with other children, and to develop a better understanding of the world around them. Outdoor play areas can also provide a safe, supportive atmosphere in which children can challenge themselves. In the following chapter, we will look at the developmental characteristics of young children that should be considered when designing the outdoor play space.

2 Developmental Characteristics of Young Children

The Whole Child

We can all agree that playgrounds should be designed to promote the healthy development of the *whole* child. We recognize that children do not discard their emotional, social, and cognitive selves during outdoor time. Children playing outside are *thinking, feeling, social, physical* beings, and their well-being must be respected on the playground as in the rest of the learning environment. To better understand children's overall development, it is useful to examine each of the developmental domains, with the understanding that these domains are interconnected. An understanding of the basic tenets of child development can guide our observations of children as they engage in outdoor play and help us make wise decisions about the way in which we design their play spaces.

There are four basic areas of development: **physical**—large body movements and fine-motor skills, **emotional**—feelings and the expression of them, **social**—interactions with others, and **cognitive**—problem solving and intellectual skills.

> As children play they offer suggestions, build on each other's ideas, and negotiate differences—all of which requires considerable cognitive and social skill.
>
> **KATZ & McCLELLAN, 1997, p. 42**

Help children break up challenges into smaller steps ... we often put the most challenging items on the playground so that children will not be bored, but this gives them little opportunity to develop the prerequisite skills.

Physical Growth and Development[1]

Physical growth, like all aspects of development, is sequential, but at any given time a specific skill area may become the focus of a child's efforts. The child will gradually gain mastery of a new skill through much practice and trial and error. For example, physical development may progress faster than cognitive development for a period of time and then plateau as social skill development occurs. Adults, through careful child observation and appropriate interaction, should be able to recognize, support, and extend the wide variation in skills and abilities of the children in their care both indoors and outside. The challenge of the early childhood play space is to provide for the appropriate practice of emerging skills while encouraging the use of mastered ones. In designing the outdoor play space, the following general **stages of physical growth** should be considered and should guide adults as they support young children's play. Remember, however, that these stages will often overlap in terms of an individual child's level of development.

First year. This first year of life marks the most significant changes that will ever occur in a child's physical abilities. It is a remarkable progression. The infant begins life in a prone position, then gradually moves to sitting to crawling to standing and cruising along furniture. Finally the first steps are taken—short, head-forward steps that are often very erratic. By 12 to 15 months, the child has usually achieved enough balance to walk unaided.

One to two years. By about 15 months the child's steps are longer and the child is able to move sideways and backwards. The child will be able to rock in a rocking chair, climb onto objects, and play on a spring-based toy. Although the child can climb stairs (sometimes in a prone position), adult support may be required for descent. A play space that includes children of this age could have handholds and railings that the toddler can grasp with both hands. Such devices will help a young climber balance while supporting his or her

---

[1]Information in this section used with permission from *The Early Childhood Playground: An Outdoor Classroom*, by S. Esbensen, 1987, Ypsilanti, MI: High/Scope Press.

attempts to master this important physical skill. The child's upright postural control improves during this period of development, and walking reflects both a newly gained confidence and a maturing body.

Two years. By the age of 2, children can turn corners when they walk. Their movement is constant and hurried. They can successfully negotiate stairs without assistance. Open, uncluttered spaces are a welcome relief for the adults caring for these active toddlers! One of the most important physical skills achieved at this age is running. Two-year-olds love using their newly acquired speed but often do not have the cognitive awareness to avoid obstacles that suddenly appear in their path. For instance, a playground risk to children at this age is being hit by a swing because they cannot judge the speed and timing accurately enough to move out of harm's way. Therefore, locate swings along the periphery of the play space and out of major traffic areas.

Toddlers begin using alternate hand and leg movements and will be curious about ladders, which are part of many play structures. A 2½-year-old child can jump from a height of 8–10 inches (20–26 cm) and still maintain his or her balance on landing. Using slides can be challenging for them, how-ever. If the slope is too steep, children at this age may lose their balance and topple backward. Toddlers and younger preschoolers will need smaller, less steep slides with safety siding and may need an adult close by.

Three years. By the age of 3, walking and running skills are well established. New skills include walking backward and controlling the stop after running. Balance and coordination are improving, enabling children to combine simple skills (run and throw, jump and clap). Children's confidence grows, and they begin to climb high-er on structures. A 3-year-old can ride a trike but is still learning to steer around objects or people. A path that allows easy passage for

Young preschoolers enjoy exploring new ways to climb.

more than one vehicle moving in opposite directions will reduce unnecessary conflict and crashes. Galloping and one-foot skipping also appear at this stage, and many 3-year-olds can throw a ball and jump off low platforms.

Four years. By the age of 4, children are learning to pump on swings by making their arms and legs move in a synchronized motion. They enjoy moving their bodies in space by whirling, jumping, swinging, turning on bars, and doing somersaults. Movements of different parts of the body are further mastered and coordinated. They can stand on one foot and walk across a low balance beam. Four-year-olds enjoy jumping on a small trampoline and will move through a multi-level modular structure in an organized fashion. They can run smoothly at different speeds and can stop and go quickly.

Five years. The 5-year-old child perfects movements that were mastered at age 4. Speed and endurance increase. Their hands and feet are well coordinated: they can shift weight from one limb to the next in a controlled manner (leading to hand-over-hand activities), they can skip with both feet, and they are able to kick a soccer ball in a specific direction up to 8 feet. Five-year-olds can climb and descend ladders and long stairways unassisted and may be able to ride a two-wheeled bike. With 5-year-olds' newly acquired social skills, games with simple rules begin to appear in play. Adult support during these games can provide the assistance children need to keep the games inclusive and rewarding. Activities with larger groups of children add challenge and social participation to their physical play.

Six to eight years. Gains in height and weight slow down at this stage of physical development. Organized games with rules, such as soccer, baseball, and other ball-based activities, are prevalent. Rough-and-tumble play and competition among children increase. Girls' and boys' play patterns are visibly different, and their play is often segregated. For boys at this age, suggest and support activities that test strength *and* require negotiation. As girls become more interested in role play and social relationships, encourage them to link these activities with upper-body challenges.

Older preschoolers begin to be interested in simple goal-directed activities.

Emotional Development

The emotional development of children is often difficult to track because it is predominantly an internal process. Children begin life with a simple set of emotions; as they develop, these emotions gradually differentiate and children experience and express more complex feelings. Their emotions, like those of adults, are based both on internal states and external events.

Outside play has an important role in the emotional development of children. Without the constraints of walls and ceilings, children are free to run, shout, and play exuberantly. Outside, children express a wide range of emotions and gain the satisfaction of solving physical and social problems as they engage in self-directed activity. In an emotionally safe, adult-supported outdoor play area, children learn that they can face, master, or alter their feelings. With new evidence supporting the link between emotional intelligence, academic success, and social acceptance, children need the opportunities that outdoor play provides to develop these important skills and strategies (Goleman, 1995).

Children's emotional growth occurs in a typical progression of stages, which is outlined by Berk (1997), below. Keep in mind that, as with other areas of development, these stages tend to overlap.

Two years and under. These youngest children are beginning to develop a sense of self—an identity independent of others. By two, the child can distinguish intentional from unintentional acts and can be quite assertive in getting something he or she wants. However, the first outward signs of empathy are evident at this stage as well. Creating an outdoor space that allows for independent exploration while creating a sense of security is important for meeting the emotional needs of this age group.

Three to four years. Children of this age experience complex emotions like shame, guilt, embarrassment, and aggression. Friendships begin to form. Use of the pronoun "I" increases, and by this time children have developed a set of feelings about themselves.

In a world that is often adult directed, the playground should be a child-friendly place.

Children may hide from unhappy situations by withdrawing, denying that a problem exists, or blaming someone else. Fears of unknown situations may cause strong emotional reactions in children. In designing a play space for this age group, provide opportunities for observation and reflection, such as observation "towers" or spring toys.

Five to six years. Children have the ability to interpret, predict, and influence others' emotions at this age. The child relies more on language rather than actions to express empathy. Both self-confidence and confidence in others increase, and although children still depend on adults for security, they are more independent. At this stage, play spaces should allow increased room for autonomous movement and creative use of loose props. Challenging climbing equipment and materials for building are other ways to meet 5- and 6-year-olds' needs.

Six to eight years. The 6- to 8-year-old child's self-worth is determined by feelings of competence and performance in specific situations. The child begins to distinguish between ability, effort, and luck in assessing the success or failure of an activity or experience. Guilt is associated with personal responsibility. This age marks the beginning of formal games with rules on the playground. Adults can help reduce negative social experiences by keeping games as cooperatively based as possible and encouraging good sportsmanship.

We want outdoor playtime to contribute to a child's sense of accomplishment and self-confidence. In play, whether indoors or outside, children should be able to express themselves in ways that reduce tension and anxiety and allow them to gain control of their lives. They do this by solving their own problems, expressing their feelings and intentions, and interacting with others in personally meaningful ways—always under the careful observation of supportive adults.

Social Development

Parten's (1932) social play theory outlines five general stages of play. In general, as children's cognitive and language skills mature they become increasingly involved with other children in play. Thus, young children move from playing mostly alone to interacting with their peers in a group. Remember, however, that children of any age may exhibit these different social play patterns according to their own needs at any particular time. Even older children and adults demonstrate solitary social behavior, and some infants appear to have a play sequence that includes characteristics of associative play (Esbensen, 1987).

The particular developmental needs of each stage of social play suggest considerations for playground design. A developmental play space will incorporate these design considerations in order to meet the needs of *all* children.

Solitary play. Children 2 and under typically spend most of their time playing alone, seemingly unaware of others. Balls, cardboard boxes, push toys, spring toys, riding toys, and low, wide ramps are appropriate items for children at this stage, with adults nearby to support them and keep them safe.

Onlooker play. At this stage children may struggle with issues of dependence and separateness and often choose to simply watch others. Provide space for observation by setting up perch points, such as rocks, spring toys, or small benches, and cozy nooks and corners that allow children to comfortably view others without having to get involved.

Parallel play. This is the most typical play pattern of 2- to 5-year-olds. In this stage of development, children play with similar materials alongside one another. While they may not try to influence the behavior of others, children at this stage do watch and imitate one another and adults. Positioning spring toys in groupings of two or three, having separate seating space in a sandbox, and providing duplicates of the same toy encourage children to engage in an activity in which others are involved as well.

Associative play. Older preschoolers will interact with their peers mostly by exchanging toys and comments but also by joining in simple games and group activities. Props that can be used in a number of ways can encourage group play at this stage.

Cooperative play. By the end of early childhood children are spending more time working with others toward a common goal and engaging in more complex interactions. For example, children will play together for longer time periods and will plan play scenarios together. Also, children at this stage engage in more turn taking and

One of the primary roles of the playground is to provide a *social* context in which children can play, learn, and develop.

Provide space and materials outdoors to support both solitary and group play.

reciprocity in their dealings with others. By accommodating all these stages of development and supporting both solitary and cooperative learning experiences, adults will be able to observe individual children carefully and support them at their particular stage of development. Regardless of children's ages or stages, the playground should provide an area where children can exercise new and emerging competencies in a social context. Their ability to handle conflict, build relationships, and express their needs will be tested and practiced. If you ask adults about their most vivid playground memories, they often will recount a specific situation or challenge that involved social interactions. Clearly, the playground is a valuable resource for socializing children as they engage in playful activities at their own developmental levels.

Cognitive Development

Understanding how children think and the manner in which they process information at different levels of development is critical to creating appropriate and rewarding outdoor play experiences. Piaget's (1952) theory of cognitive development, established through extensive observation of children, offers a framework for understanding how young children learn.

Sensorimotor stage. Infants and toddlers "think" by acting on the world with their mouths, eyes, ears, and hands. Cognition and physical development are closely linked, and if physical skills are impaired, cognition can also be affected. Therefore, infants and toddlers need their own safe outdoor space in which to sit, explore, crawl, walk, and climb without being "run over" by older children. As adults well know, infants and young toddlers will put most things into their mouths after an initial visual inspection. This means that adults should bring out loose materials children can safely handle and mouth; they should also ensure that nearby vegetation is nontoxic (see Appendix C, p. 94).

Preoperational stage. This stage is characterized by symbolic thinking and continued learning through experience. Preschoolers learn to use words, objects, and pictures as *symbols* standing for other objects or ideas, hence the increase in language skills and imaginative play. However, a child's intellectual reasoning is intuitive and based on appearances rather than on logic, as an adult's or older child's is.

Between **2 and 3 years** of age, children become aware of the difference between their inner thoughts and external events. Their vocabulary increases rapidly, and they begin to demonstrate reciprocity in conversation. Children learn to organize and classify objects in their world based on a similar feature. Therefore children need places for conversation (side-by-side swings, tire swing, benches) and loose materials to organize and transport.

By **3 to 4 years** of age, children have gained a basic understanding of causality. They use self-talk to guide behavior when working on challenging tasks and are able to generalize information from one situation to another. By this age, children also develop an understanding of how objects relate to each other, how parts join together to make a whole, and how objects are arranged in space in relation to each other. They can tell which of two things is bigger or smaller, and objects can be understood in terms of their amount. Children can now classify objects based on more than one attribute. Therefore, for example, children would benefit from climbers with parts they can move and reassemble in a variety of ways.

By **5 to 6 years,** children's ability to distinguish fantasy from reality improves, and their play becomes more involved and complex. There is an increased ability to group objects according to important characteristics, such as color, shape, size, and function. At this age children enjoy "wild" places to explore and map out their own interpretations of, for example, fairy tales and shipwrecks.

Concrete operational stage. By 6 to 8 years of age, children's thinking and reasoning skills become more logical, although learning remains tied to concrete experiences. They are able to understand spatial concepts and are improving their ability to judge distance, time, and speed. Attention becomes more focused and planning skills, more involved. Their language continues to focus on concrete functions and attributes. Children at this age need space and equipment for games of skill such as croquet, hockey, and softball.

Manipulative materials allow children to create, pretend, and participate at a variety of developmental levels.

Understanding the various stages of children's cognitive development is as important for playground designers as understanding all other developmental areas. As we stress throughout this chapter, all developmental areas are interrelated and all must be considered in establishing learning environments—including the outdoor space—for young children. For this reason, Piaget's aforementioned stages of cognitive development provide a useful set of guidelines for creating an outdoor play space that offers children plentiful opportunities for fun *and* learning.

Sensory Experiences Outdoors

Since young children learn by using *all* their senses, outdoor play environments should offer a variety of sensory experiences. Ayres (1979) emphasizes that the more experiences children have with their senses, the more knowledge they gain. The following sensory areas should be considered when designing outdoor play spaces for young children: **visual, vestibular, kinesthetic, tactile, auditory,** and **taste.**

Visual Sense

In playground design, the visual sense is often overlooked because adults tend to focus more on functional requirements and practical considerations. Yet active play environments should provide as much visual variety as possible—interesting shapes, colors, and forms. This makes the play space more inviting and stimulating and also helps to improve spatial perception.

Vestibular Sense

The vestibular system consists of small, liquid-filled tubes in the inner ear and is important in maintaining a child's sense of balance. The movement of liquid through these canals produces stimulation of the nervous system. Sensory experiences change every time the head moves in a different direction or at a different speed; this explains children's great enjoyment of whirling or being tossed in the air. During their first years, children's vestibular systems are very receptive to even small amounts of stimulation, and slight variations in speed and direction have a substantial effect on balance. The vestibular system works with the senses of touch and vision as well as sensations from the joints and muscles to help children orient themselves in space. When children go down a slide, for example, they both feel and see themselves moving downward through space. By about the age of 8, the sensory-motor development of children is well established.

Kinesthetic Sense

The kinesthetic sense detects body position, weight, and movement of the muscles, tendons, and joints. This sense influences children's eye-hand and eye-foot coordination. Children develop spatial awareness by using their bodies to experiment with the relationship of self to the environment. You can give children opportunities to do this by providing equipment and materials for them to climb on, crawl under, jump over, and hang from. Children also like to hide in small spaces, crouch in corners, and squeeze backwards through holes as they experiment with moving their bodies in many different ways.

Tactile Sense

The tactile sense involves the entire surface of the body as children experience changes in texture and temperature through their sense of touch. In the outdoor setting, nature alone provides children with a great variety of interesting textures to explore. Building snow sculptures, digging in dirt, rolling in grass, and tending a garden provide excellent opportunities for children to gain an appreciation of the natural world through their sense of touch. Weather conditions also provide natural tactile sensa-

Nature provides an array of sensory experiences—sight, touch, movement, and taste.

tions as children feel the rush of the wind, the warmth of the sun, or the nip of the cold on their skin. You can extend and enrich children's tactile explorations by providing water, sand, and other sensory materials.

Auditory Sense

The outdoor setting provides an array of sounds if only we take the time to listen. Help children focus on and identify the different sounds around them, such as children shouting, cars honking, equipment rattling, dogs barking, birds chirping, and leaves crunching underfoot. Children's auditory experience is enhanced as they hear and listen for new sounds in the outdoors. Children should also be encouraged to use their voices outside. Outdoor play gives them plenty of opportunity to sing, shout, or make whatever noises they wish.

A successful playground facilitates the development of the *whole* child.

Sense of Taste

Children, especially toddlers and younger preschoolers, are very curious about the taste of the outdoors; it is natural for them to want to chomp on twigs or take a first sip of mud soup. Adults must therefore watch children carefully to make sure that they are not harmed by these explorations. Adults also need to make sure that there are no toxins washing into the earth and that poisonous plants are not in the immediate play environment.

Summary

Considering developmental stages and characteristics of children of different ages when designing a playground will help to ensure that it is appropriate for a range of abilities and interests—all of which have been described in this chapter. In the next chapter, we explore the various areas that are important to include in playground design.

3 Playground Design

You have likely taken great care in designing your interior space to maximize learning and social interaction. By carefully planning your outdoor environment, you will likewise ensure a design that matches your goals for children's outside play.

There are several steps in the design process:

- Clarifying the purpose of your outdoor space
- Analyzing children's outdoor play patterns and needs
- Assessing the outdoor environment
- Planning the layout

> While educators typically devote ample time and energy to organizing and equipping their classrooms, they often overlook the importance of the . . . playground.
>
> **HARRIS, 1991, p. 167**

Clarifying the Purpose of Your Outdoor Space

Before furnishing your playground, it is important to establish the basic objectives of your outdoor play space. Like the indoor space, it should reflect the values and philosophy of the general program. Answering the following questions will help you design an outdoor area that best fits the needs of your children.

What Are the Objectives of Your Outdoor Environment?

- Encourage interaction with and respect for nature
- Provide variety in the curriculum
- Allow a space for release of energy
- Challenge children's physical abilities

- Encourage cooperative social play
- Foster autonomy and initiative
- Integrate children with special needs
- Promote language skills
- Foster creativity
- Provide opportunities for children to problem solve
- Encourage multi-age play
- Foster child-adult interaction
- Other objectives: _____

Are the Objectives of Your Outdoor Environment Consistent With Your Overall Program Philosophy?

Both the indoor and outdoor environments should make the same statement to children about what is important. For instance, if social play is emphasized in your program, you will want to provide both indoor and outdoor activities that encourage children to work and play together.

In What Ways Can the Outdoor Playground Setting Best Supplement the Indoor Learning Environment?

Bringing inside materials and activities out to the playground often sparks new interest in them and provides an opportunity for different ways of experimenting with them. However, the playground should also provide a change of pace from inside exploration. Make it a place where children can roam freely, play hard, and be noisy.

Analyzing Children's Outdoor Play Patterns and Needs

Once you understand what it is you want your playground to provide, observe how the children use your present space. This will give you an idea of what is working, what needs to be changed, and whether the goals of your program are achievable in the current space. If you don't yet have your own playground, visit another center's.

There are two primary ways to observe children outside. The first is to keep a running record of an individual child's play patterns.

The early childhood playground should be considered an extension of the classroom. . . .
ESBENSEN, 1987, p. 10

Follow one child for a period of 5, 10, or 15 minutes. Document his or her movements, interactions with peers, and the quality of the play—creative, social, cognitive, physical. You could also do a short running record of one child over two or three days. If possible, have other staff members keep running records on different children.

The second method involves observing the children as a group. Note their movement patterns over the whole space and listen for the general tone of their voices. Observe the kinds of interactions that occur among the children and between the teachers and children. Are the adults able to interact with children while maintaining a view of the entire playground? Also, note which equipment is used and whether it fits the children's needs. For group observation, use the Qualitative Playground Observation Record form in Appendix A, p. 85.

Your notes will provide a great deal of information about the child-play space fit. With your team members, use these observations to clarify the purpose of the playground and to further your efforts to use this space to promote children's learning and overall development. Your play-space design and equipment will then be an accurate reflection of your program philosophy.

With brushes and a bucket of water, children enjoy a new canvas for painting!

Multi-age Play Outdoors

Children of different ages play together in families and in many child care situations as well, particularly in family day cares or other centers that offer after-school programs for school-aged children. These mixed-age groupings allow interaction between children of a wide variety of developmental levels, a situation which can extend and enrich children's play.

For safety reasons, the American Society for Testing and Materials (ASTM) recommends separate outdoor play spaces for 2- to 5-year-olds and 5- to 12-year-olds. This might be accomplished by placing fences, shrubs, or benches between areas. However, this may not be feasible for some programs due to space, equipment, or staffing limitations. If you have a wide span of ages sharing your outdoor space, it is important to ensure everyone's safety by providing equipment that is appropriate for all users and by having adequate supervision. A variety of loose manipulative materials (see Chapter 4) can help make your playground usable and enjoyable for children of all ages.

It is also important to determine the needs of the children who will be using the site. Will the space mainly be used by infants and toddlers, preschoolers, or children in after-school care? If it is a multi-age program, do you have space for separate play areas? How many children will use the space, and what will the ratio be of children to adults? Will any special considerations be necessary for children or staff with mobility impairments or assistive devices?

Assessing the Outdoor Environment

Good design of a play environment involves balancing program values, children's needs, and site conditions. As you view your site, think about the type of space you are working with:

- Type and amount of natural materials
- A very small or very large space
- Topographical elements such as a steep slope or a big tree stump in the middle of the space
- Shared space with another program
- A roof deck with an unbreakable waterproof membrane
- An extremely noisy setting

The Playground Site

A helpful way of assessing your present space is to draw a rough diagram. The following steps will help you do this. Photographs may also be helpful in capturing subtleties such as sunlight patterns or hidden nooks and crannies.

Step one. Measure your site and determine the scale for your drawing. With north at the top of the page, draw one element on the site as a focal point.

Step two. Identify all other existing elements on the site. Pathways, trees, shrubs, fencing, buildings, large rocks, and any other permanent and semi-permanent features should be noted. You can sketch a bubble diagram like that shown on the following page to outline the shapes and still keep the notation to scale.

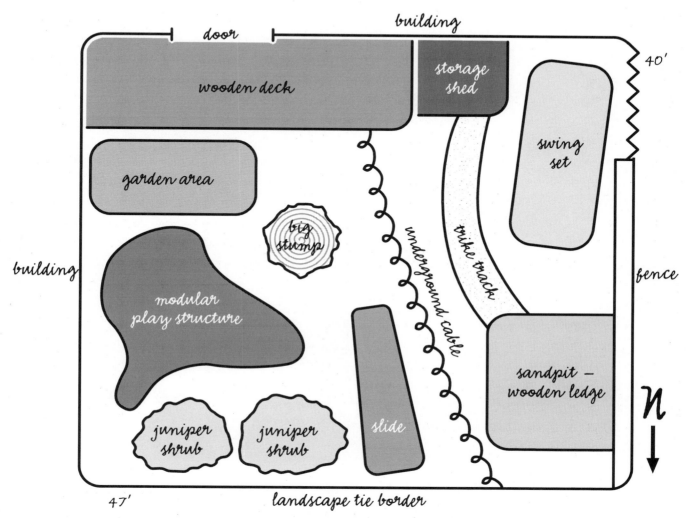

Bubble Diagram for Assessing a Space

Step three. Identify the plants and trees present and check that all are nontoxic (see Appendix C, p. 94).

Step four. Note any areas particularly affected by sun, shade, wind, rain, and snow.

Step five. Locate any underground services, such as sewer, water, and gas. Are there any overhead power or phone lines? Is

Whenever possible, incorporate the natural elements of your space into play design. The large tree on this playground provides a perfect base for a tree house.

there an overhanging roof or tree branch? If your play space is on a rooftop, can equipment be attached to the surface? What is the allowable weight load?

Step six. Look over the topography of the area. Indicate any natural slopes or valleys.

Step seven. Identify any drainage problems on the playground.

Step eight. Determine if there is any connection to water for play activities.

The Surrounding Community

Next, look beyond your immediate play area to the surrounding environment with these questions in mind:

- What is the character of the surrounding community? Is it industrial, rural, or inner city? Does it include many different cultures?

- Can this space reflect the values of the neighborhood? How? For instance, in a predominantly aboriginal village in northern British Columbia where community and cooperation are highly valued, the outdoor space, equipment, and activities promote these ideals.

- What play structures are already available for children? For example, does the local park already have tire swings and a fire engine? You might want to avoid exact duplicates of local playgrounds' equipment.

- What can your outdoor space provide that may be lacking in children's homes or community environments?

- How will your outdoor space be affected by other neighborhood conditions including traffic patterns, residential units, businesses, and so on? Do these have implications for safety, acceptable levels of noise, hours of operation, and other considerations?

Operational Aspects

In addition to assessing the overall environment, the following issues need to be addressed:

- How will the project be financed?
- What are the zoning requirements? What permits are needed?
- What are the sources for ordering or obtaining equipment and materials?
- Who will install and maintain the playground?
- Who will do the landscaping?

If your center has limited space for outdoor play, or if you simply want some variety in your routine, take children to a nearby public park along with loose manipulatives and toys to ride on.

Climate Considerations

When planning your outdoor space, it is important to consider the impact of climate and weather conditions on outdoor activities. Some climates are characterized by extreme seasonal changes, while others are moderate year-round. Planning an all-season playground will make your space more usable and enhance children's enjoyment of the outdoors. Some natural elements to consider are outlined here.

Sunlight

Observe the areas of your outdoor space that are exposed to direct and indirect light and the areas that are shaded. Materials such as asphalt, concrete, cast iron, and steel may absorb too much heat and be uncomfortable surfaces for children. If you do use these materials, try to place them in areas that are shaded during the hot parts of the day and year. Materials such as wood, rope, grass, and some kinds of plastic are better choices for hot climates and may help prevent serious burns. Children may need trees, awnings, and building overhangs to protect them from too much exposure. Direct sunlight is important, however, for plant growth and for sterilizing sand and water. Your play space should have varying levels of exposure to direct sunlight.

Wind

Although a cool breeze is welcomed on a hot day, chilly winds often limit outdoor play time. To minimize wind hazards, determine in which direction your winter winds blow. If winds are frequently severe enough to affect outdoor play, plan wind breaks on your playground. Upright structural devices such as fences or securely fastened sheds can be helpful, as can natural breaks like trees and shrubs.

Rain

Rain is as much a part of life in some regions as snow is in others, and children are fascinated by rain—especially puddles! Properly attired—in raincoats, plastic pants, boots, and with an extra set of clothing handy—children must have the opportunity to play in wet weather. On those days when it really is impractical to play on the playground, providing a sheltered area or protected play structure close to the building could still allow children some outdoor time.

Snow provides a medium for exploring new ways to move!

Take advantage of rainy days in other ways, too, such as collecting rain in child-made gauges or watching what happens when rain falls on paper that has powdered paint on it.

Ice and snow

If you live in a region with a lot of snow, plan your space to take advantage of it. Elevate play structures (ensuring that summertime resilient surfacing underneath is adequate) to allow for snow buildup. (If your play space is fenced in, remember to plan gate widths that will allow snow removal equipment to access the area.) One preschool in the northern part of British Columbia had snow and ice tunnels that linked the lower portions of play structures. Ice and snow had built up on platforms and the children made ice castles and other creations with it. In a Yukon village where snow was on the ground 10 months of the year, the snow was used as resilient surfacing underneath play structures because of its depth and absorbency.

At an elementary school in small-town Saskatchewan, the principal herself supervises outside play time when the temperature reaches minus 31 degrees Fahrenheit (minus 35 degrees Celsius).

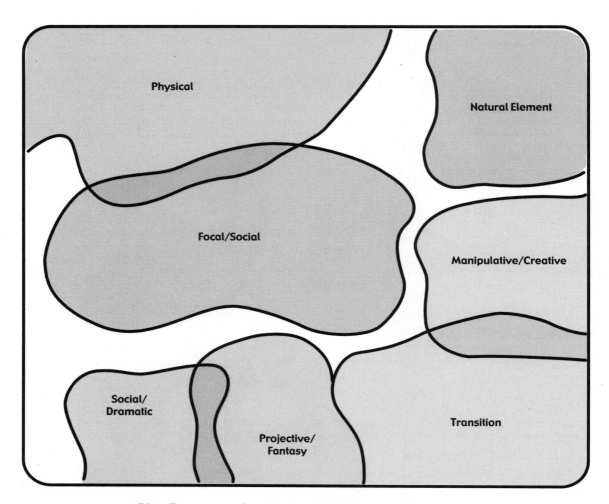

Physical

Natural Element

Focal/Social

Manipulative/Creative

Social/
Dramatic

Projective/
Fantasy

Transition

Play Zones on a Sample Family Child Care Playground

Children who go outside ten times during the year in that cold become members of the Polar Bear Club, a prestigious designation in the school. Learn to celebrate the unique elements of *your* area!

Planning the Layout

Before choosing the actual equipment for your playground, it is helpful to have an overall plan or design for the placement of furnishings. You will want to organize the space in a way that will promote physical and social play while minimizing conflicts. While there are many ways to do this, there is one method for organizing the outdoor play space that has been successfully implemented in a variety of settings. This method, outlined by Esbenson in his book *The Early Childhood Playground: An Outdoor Classroom* (1987), is called the zoned approach.

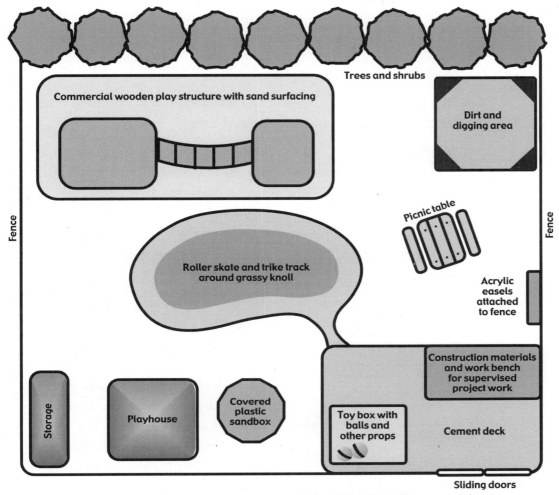

Satellite Play Areas on Sample Family Child Care Playground

The Zoned Approach

Similar to the way a classroom is arranged into specific areas or centers—the art area, block area, house area, etc.—small groupings of functionally separate outdoor play areas called *zones* can enrich children's interactions with the equipment, nature, adults, and one another. Instead of having one large, central structure that attempts to provide a variety of experiences and activities for children, each zone includes several smaller, related activities and pieces of equipment (see zone and satellite diagrams above). This allows more active play areas to be separated from areas that involve less noisy creative or manipulative activities, and can help minimize the tendency for louder, bigger boys to dominate a play structure (Boulton, 1992). Esbensen outlines seven distinct yet overlapping zones, each focusing on a particular type of play. As you read the description of each zone, refer to the sample diagrams presented here.

Transition zone

The transition zone is the area between your building and the playground or between different play zones. This area allows children time and space to decide where they want to go as they enter the playground. The transition zone can be an open space, or it can offer quiet activities such as a water table or seating area with table and chairs.

Manipulative/creative zone

Although the playground is traditionally thought of as a place for large-motor activities, fine-motor activities can also be promoted outside. The manipulative/creative zone might include a table filled with sand or rice, an easel with paints, or a table set up with clay or markers. A carefully supervised construction area with small hammers, nails, and wood pieces would also be very appealing to children. This type of area could provide a place for children to make projects with natural materials, such as stringing berries on a piece of yarn. A Plexiglas easel attached to a fence or wall

A quiet retreat offers these girls a place to enjoy a tasty treat together.

and a space for block building are also good examples of materials that would foster creative outdoor experiences.

Projective/fantasy zone

The projective/fantasy zone is filled with materials to fuel children's imaginations: crates of plastic animals, a wheeled outdoor cupboard with stacks of blocks, and buckets of toy bulldozers, trucks, and cars. Locate water and sand nearby to increase the richness of this play.

Focal/social zone

Although the playground is a place of action, there should also be a place that fosters a sense of community, a place where children can sit and talk with their peers, share a discovery with an adult, or simply observe. Picnic tables, a bench, an old tree stump, and large stones can make an inviting setting for discussion, observation, and quiet retreat.

Social/dramatic zone

Dramatic play offers children a safe arena in which to try out new roles or work out difficult feelings. A furnished playhouse, a play car with hand gears, and an elevated platform for a fort can stimulate all kinds of language and social play. In addition to such traditional props as a table, chairs, and a kitchen set in the playhouse, bring other materials outside from time to time. For example, to transform the playhouse into a fire station, you could add a couple of firefighter hats, a noisemaker for a siren, and some red raincoats. Also, with an old white sheet thrown over the top of the playhouse, children could create a secret hideaway or a haunted house.

In addition to specific costumes or dress-up clothes, provide several scarves and large pieces of fabric for children to create their own ensembles.

Physical zone

The physical zone provides space for activities that are difficult to accommodate indoors. Children can develop climbing skills, strengthen their muscles, and improve balance and coordination. The equipment in this zone, like the others, should allow for many different uses and stimulate the imagination as well as encourage physical activity. (Specific equipment will be discussed in the following chapter.) Plan open areas, too, as some of the best physical activity—running, walking, jumping, rolling—requires no equipment.

The physical zone should include open space for a chase!

In addition, a bike path can furnish hours of fun for children using wheelbarrows, wagons, pull toys, scooters, and tricycles.

It is important that equipment in this area be scaled to the size and ability level of the children using it. If children of different ages will use the same equipment, be sure that it is appropriate for all. A general rule is that children should be able to access play equipment by themselves, although children with special needs may require adult assistance to utilize equipment. If structures are so high that children need assistance, they could fall and sustain a serious injury.

Natural element zone

Sand, grass, nontoxic plants, flowers, and trees are an important part of children's outdoor exploration, and certainly your entire outdoor space should contain a variety of natural elements. You might plan a particular area, however, that offers some special nature experiences—dirt to dig in or grow plants, tall grass and flowers to attract insects, a rock garden to explore.

It is important to remember that "learning about the world of nature is not a frill" (Wilson, Kilmer, & Knauerhase, 1996, p. 56). Though it may seem convenient to cut down a particular tree or flatten a slope to make room for equipment for children to play on, this denies children the opportunity to learn about and develop a sense of responsibility and respect for the world around them. Replacement of nature with manufactured materials may also be contributing to children's dislike for the natural environment. Bixler, Carlisle, Hammitt, and Floyd (1994) found that children living in urban areas frequently use words like "diseased," "disgusting," and "dirty" to describe different aspects of nature, and they are surprisingly fearful of plants and insects. It is essential that we encourage children's active exploration of the natural environment. Says Blow (1996, p. 4), "Child's play is so clean it's a dirty shame. Whatever happened to mud pies and digging to China?" It is important to provide areas in the playground where children can experience nature in meaningful and direct ways.

Layout Considerations

The layout of a playground can have a significant impact on the quality of children's play. Here are some general considerations for locating play areas:

- Organize zones to facilitate play and minimize conflicts (for example, locate quiet play areas away from more active spaces).

- Provide areas that encourage group interaction as well as places for solitary and partner play.

- Avoid putting high-activity zones close to transitional zones.

- If possible, locate compatible play zones close together. For example, creative play and social play could be adjacent to each other.

- Design all play zones for child-initiated activity.

- Locate play areas for toddlers and areas involving quiet, creative activities near the entry to the building.

- Use low, natural partitions and different surfacing materials to define zones (pea gravel under swings, wood borders around the edge of the sandbox, for instance).

- Use space wisely, leaving some areas open. A cluttered playground detracts from children's explorations and can cause conflicts.

- Plan zones to take advantage of any prominent or unusual elements. For example, locate the physical zone around a slope designed for running or sledding.

- Be sure that equipment and landscaping do not interfere with visual supervision. Adults must be able to scan the entire playground.

- If at all possible, retain existing trees, shrubs, and other landscaping.

- Locate the play area away from dumpsters, heavy traffic, and loud noises. If you have no choice about where to locate the play area, ameliorate the effects of smells, noise, and other distractions by planting or building camouflages and auditory or visual barriers such as trees, shrubs, or wooden fences.
- Make sure the site is accessible for maintenance and emergency equipment.
- Use your imagination. Paint stones, create a mural, make handprints in cement. Cue children through the color, shape, and type of materials that this is their place to play. Involve the children in designing and creating these distinctive elements.

Summary

Designing the outdoor play space involves carefully assessing your site and planning a layout that will fit the physical space and the needs of the children in your program. The zoned approach can help you provide a balanced play site. Keep in mind this need for balance as we look at equipment options in the next chapter. Modular structures can merge different kinds of play into one unit and can be especially useful in small, limited spaces. For example, you can find playhouses with ladders going up to the roof, and elevated sand play structures that children climb up to, using pulleys to draw up buckets and shovels. Many of the larger play structures incorporate social seating, sand play, and creative and manipulative activities. If a modular structure is used, make sure that children have opportunities to engage in natural play experiences as well. We will look next at how to furnish your outdoor classroom with items that meet your program's goals and objectives for children.

4 Furnishing the Outdoor Classroom

Since our basic goal when furnishing the outdoor classroom is to optimize learning while providing enjoyable play experiences for children, the structures chosen for this area are very important. When considering equipment choices, keep in mind that there are two basic categories of outdoor equipment: *stationary structures* and *loose manipulative materials*. Both types of equipment can be used to facilitate children's active explorations and discoveries and are the major topics of this chapter.

Stationary Structures

This category includes large-motor equipment typically seen on most playgrounds: swings, climbers, slides, etc. A wide variety of attractive modular play equipment is available commercially, but remember that the natural resources you may already have can also provide exciting opportunities for climbing, sliding, and jumping. Do you have good climbing trees? Or trees that could support swing ropes? How about a large boulder or a few large stones for jumping over and off of? Balancing on logs, climbing on stumps, and rolling down hills (which you could even make yourself with some help) are all natural ways for children to expand their skills.

> A piece of play equipment has play value when adult educational objectives are successfully disguised as something children would like to do for fun.
>
> **M.T. JENSEN, 1992, personal communication**

When purchasing playground equipment, particularly large climbing structures, you will find that most pieces are made of wood, steel, plastic, or fiberglass. As you assess materials, look for durability, ease of maintenance, and perhaps a mixture of different materials and colors. Children generally prefer bright colors but are also attracted to wooden structures that "fit in" with the natural surroundings. One strategy might be to use bright colors to identify active play areas and more muted, natural tones to identify quiet play areas (tree stumps and rocks in the focal/social zone, for instance). Whatever material, color, or type of equipment is chosen, it should be inviting for young children, provide opportunities for open-ended, child-initiated play, and be safe for children to use.

The equipment you consider for your playground must, of course, fit in the space you have available. If your space is very limited, you may need to choose one to three small stationary structures and supplement them with loose toys and props (see pp. 45–49).

Climbing Structures

The focal point of most playgrounds, climbers come in all shapes and sizes. A climber can be as simple as a tree stump, rock, or stairs leading to a single platform, or it can be a large composite structure of connected activities (known as a modular structure). Climbers often contain tunnels, bridges, lookout points, steering wheels, slides, and sliding poles. Children can access the different levels by using stairs, ladders, nets, or simply by hoisting themselves up. Having more than one way for children to climb up and down a structure is important, both for safety's sake and to provide challenges for children of different abilities.

Climbers do more than promote children's upper- and lower-body development. Like walking on inclined surfaces or across icy sidewalks, climbing challenges children's sense of balance and develops their ability to hold themselves upright and prevent falls. Balance is also affected by a child's center of gravity; the illustration on the opposite page shows how center of gravity changes with age and height.

Display children's plants and nature collections/creations in the playhouse.

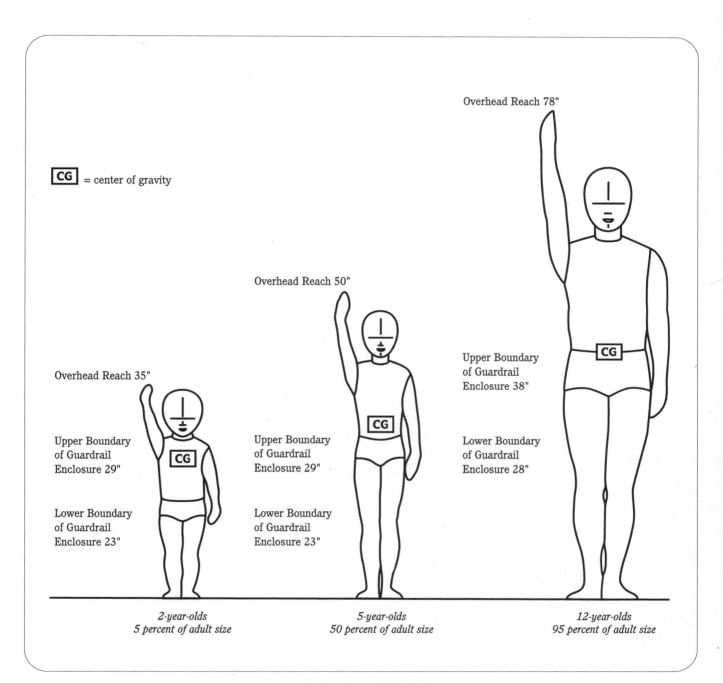

Size Comparison of Children

©NPSI. 1999. Note: Adapted from National Playground Safety Institute Certification Curriculum, National Recreation and Park Association, 1999, Ashburn, VA: NRPA. Used with permission.

Playhouses

Playhouses are one of the most important pieces of equipment in the early childhood outdoor play space. A well-designed playhouse encourages children to engage in complex imaginative and social play—acting out their experiences, interacting with peers, and trying out new ideas and identities—and to develop their language and motor skills. Remember that children will generally have richer play experiences if the playhouse is furnished, for example, with a table and chairs; shelves for storing containers of "food" made from sand, leaves, or pebbles; or other items reflecting your program's particular region or culture. Keep in mind, however, that *too* many furnishings can distract from children using their imaginations.

Swings

Swings are a favorite of children; the speed, motion, and height experienced while swinging are very stimulating to them. It can be very satisfying for older preschoolers to finally learn to pump by themselves! Although it can be time consuming for adults to push children on swings, this activity does provide an excellent opportunity for conversation between children and adults.

Horizontal tire swings offer some unique benefits to children. They can accommodate several children at once, encouraging language and social development. Because this type of tire swing moves in more than one direction, it offers children an opportunity to learn to work together.

A tire swing turns an individual experience into an opportunity for children to socialize and work together.

There are several safety concerns to consider with both traditional and tire swings, however. For those children who can pump independently, the height and speed they achieve can be dangerous both to themselves and to other children in the vicinity. For both types of swings, but especially tire swings, adult assistance may be needed to help children safely access and exit the swing. Keep in mind that swings require a great deal of space on a playground and must be placed well away from other equipment for safety. Consider excluding swings from your playground if space is an important issue for you. Swings are often found in backyards and on public playgrounds. If this is the case in your area, you would be justified in making this decision.

Slides

Children are thrilled by the sense of speed and daring they achieve by going down a slide. Either freestanding or part of a climbing structure, slides range in size from barely above the ground to several feet high. They can be straight, gently curved, or spiral (although older spiral slides can be dangerous for young children if there is not proper head clearance as children descend, the new versions are quite safe). Slides attached to climbing structures are often wide enough for two or three children to descend together, which may increase opportunities for social interaction.

Newer slides have several features that make them safer than previous models. Slides should have protective siding at the top and high side rails to prevent falls. A smooth, sloping exit close to the ground will minimize the type of injuries that often have occurred at the bottom of a slide. New standards dictate large safety zones that prevent children from accidentally colliding with other children playing nearby. Periodically check the safety surfacing at the bottom of the slide to keep it from becoming hard and packed down or worn away.

Seesaws

There are two types of seesaws: spring-based and the traditional or old-fashioned type. Traditional seesaws pose several problems for

young children. Preschoolers generally do not have the understanding necessary to make a seesaw move up and down or to coordinate their movements with another child's. Children of different weights can become frustrated by their inability to ride together, and conflicts may arise when one child is continually up and the other is down. By far the most compelling argument against old-fashioned seesaws, however, is their potential for injury, particularly to a child's head and back. This equipment simply requires more physical skill—for getting on, staying on, and getting off—than most young children possess. For these reasons, traditional seesaws should not be part of an early childhood playground.

Fortunately (because children do love the motion and height of seesaws), spring-based seesaws offer a similar yet much safer experience for young children. The spring makes it easier for two children to learn to coordinate their hands and feet in order to spring higher and bounce harder. Also, children can play alongside those of a different size, including adults. Best of all, the design of this type of seesaw reduces the risks of physical injury to children.

These spring-based seesaws replace the dangerous fulcrum-based ones of yesterday, accommodating more children and keeping them safer.

Spring Toys

One of the smallest pieces of playground equipment, spring toys allow children to rock back and forth and/or sideways at a speed they control. The toys are often shaped like animals or vehicles. Spring toys help develop balance, coordination, and muscle strength. The rocking motion can be stimulating for children who like speed, yet comforting for those who prefer to rock gently. As with swings, children gain a sense of speed and motion, yet spring toys take up little space, are generally inexpensive, and can be propelled independently by even very young children. Spring toys can be placed side by side for parallel and associative play, allowing children to be part of a social activity in a very nonthreatening way.

Spring toys are wonderful for children and adults alike!

Loose Manipulative Materials

In addition to traditional playground equipment, adding other items to outdoor time will significantly enrich children's play. Unlike stationary equipment, loose manipulatives are items that can be handled by children, are not fixed in place, and can be carried from one location to another. Some of these materials, such as sand, remain on the playground while others—wheeled toys, balls, art materials—are brought out by adults each day or for occasional use. Loose manipulatives promote open-ended, enjoyable activity that enables children to make numerous choices and decisions about their individual play experiences.

Keep in mind that young children often enjoy playing with real, adult-sized items. Especially in the case of loose manipulatives, such as props for pretend play and construction materials, real objects may be particularly appealing. When it is clear that children's preferences are for the "real thing," by all means let them play with that item, as long as it is safe for them to use.

Sand

Sandboxes are a staple of most playgrounds. Your sand play area can be at ground level, enclosed by wood to keep the sand in and debris out, or it can be elevated—a sand table, for example. Tables are particularly beneficial for children who are in wheelchairs or who find it easier to balance while standing rather than while sitting or kneeling. If you have children with these needs but only have a ground-level sandbox, adding some raised backrests may offer them the necessary support.

Sand used in play is different from the type used under equipment to absorb impacts. Play sand should be moldable, whereas safety sand needs to be looser so that it does not pack down (safety sand will be discussed further in Chapter 5). According to Esbensen (1987), sand that is used for play should

- Be 15–18 in. (38–45 cm.) deep.
- Pack down and hold its shape when wet, like seaside sand. It should hold moisture by becoming more adhesive (unlike mud or pea gravel).
- Contain a mixture of fine and coarse particles. Granules of different sizes pack together the best.
- Be free of sharp materials. Make sure that crushed stone has not been used.
- Be washed or sanitized and free of clay, oxides, and other contaminants. To test for this, place a handful of sand in a white cloth to see if it leaves stains.
- Be raked regularly for hidden hazardous objects.

In addition, your sand area should be kept covered when not in use to keep out debris and contaminants. Check the level of sand periodically, adding more sand as it gets depleted or the quality deteriorates.

In addition to commonly used sand toys, add other items to the sand area such as plastic figures, toy vehicles, blocks, kitchen play items, plastic eggs for scooping, and design tools (combs, dowels, craft sticks, half of a plastic lid with a pattern cut out of the straight edge). If water is close by, occasionally adding it to the sand will allow children to explore a different medium.

Water

Because water holds such a special attraction for children and offers rich play experiences, water play should be incorporated into every play space. Children learn important and meaningful language concepts and explore firsthand the unique properties of water when they use materials such as cups, funnels, squeeze bottles, and sponges to fill, empty, pour, and squeeze. Pretend-play materials—such as toy figures, boats, plastic dishes to wash, and dolls to bathe—provide additional enjoyment *and* learning.

Add to the fun of outdoor water play by providing a hose or a hand pump to fill basins, tubs, or the water table, and to add water to the sandbox. Provide a birdbath so children can watch birds and float twigs and feathers in the basin. To introduce water in another form, freeze colored water in plastic containers and place in the water table; children enjoy watching the giant ice cubes melt and mix colors.

Water play outdoors offers all the benefits of indoor water play, plus it allows children to explore more freely. It also provides an alternative to active, boisterous outdoor play for children who wish to engage in a calmer activity.

Wheeled Toys

Provide a wide range of vehicles for children to ride on, push, and pull. Having a variety of wheeled toys to choose from allows children to experience different gross-motor challenges at varying levels of skill. In addition to traditional tricycles and big wheel toys, provide trikes that accommodate two passengers, scooters, cars with steering wheels, wagons, strollers, and wheelbarrows. A smooth, solid surface that is located around the perimeter of the playground or away from other equipment is a must when providing riding toys. You will also need a shed or storage cabinets, preferably located outside, in which to store the vehicles.

Nature-Related Materials

Add some of these materials to your outdoor play space to help extend children's appreciation and enjoyment of nature:

- Bird feeders (can be a wonderful supervised construction project)
- Binoculars (for bird or squirrel watching)
- Compost box (another good supervised construction project)
- Birdbaths
- Wind chimes
- Flags, wind socks, or long ribbons glued to sticks
- Rain gauge
- A "watching tub" (watch it fill with snow in the winter, rain in the spring, leaves in the fall)
- Magnifying glasses (hand-held or part of a table top)
- Worm gardens (in an old aquarium)
- Dress-up clothes (park ranger, firefighter, jungle explorer)
- Thermometer (showing both Celsius and Fahrenheit)
- Water table (explore the temperature changes throughout the day)
- Raised garden beds (standing height, accessible for children using wheelchairs or standing frames)
- Garden boxes (individual for children to tend their own)
- Trees (have a tree-planting ceremony!)
- Outdoor art center (for leaf rubbings, bark tracings, collages)
- Buckets of seashells, sticks, and stones for making designs in the dirt, sand, or grass

Obstacle Courses

Using different movements to maneuver around, over, under, and through objects is an excellent way to develop children's motor planning abilities, physical skills, and movement concepts. Many items can be used to create an obstacle course, such as hoops, tires, boxes, blocks, rope, and large cardboard boxes. Children will probably be eager to suggest additional materials and new ways to set them up!

Miscellaneous Materials

Many other materials can add variety and interest to outdoor time and can stimulate children's creative and social play. For example, provide a number of different items children can use to throw, catch, bounce, roll, and dribble, such as general playground balls, beach balls, bean bags, stuffed cloth balls, and tennis balls. Building materials—such as pieces of wood, large blocks, boxes of different shapes and sizes, old tires, and sheets or blankets—can provide lots of opportunities for children to create and work together. Also, provide role-play items from the kitchen or housekeeping areas inside as well as items that have an outdoor focus, such as camping equipment or items to outfit a flower shop. For some additional ideas for outdoor materials and activities, see Appendix B, p. 89. The possibilities for outdoor fun are almost endless!

A storage locker or shed will help keep all of your portables neatly in one central area. In addition to wheeled toys and balls, fill the shed with dress-up clothes (perhaps

Paper bags filled with newspaper provide an interesting alternative to balls. These children stuffed and taped the bags themselves during indoor group time.

some bulkier items such as construction worker hard hats, plastic overcoats, and big boots) and containers of blocks, dolls, toy vehicles, and animals.

Outdoor Equipment and Activities for Children With Special Needs

There are many ways to help children with special needs participate in outdoor activities. The first issue is accessibility; make sure you have a paved area so that children using wheelchairs or walkers can get to different areas of the playground (see Chapter 5 for other accessible surfacing materials). Since the surfacing materials underneath play structures are generally not accessible, adults may need to assist children in getting to equipment such as swings or climbers, and then also assist children with using the equipment. A climbing structure or elevated playhouse

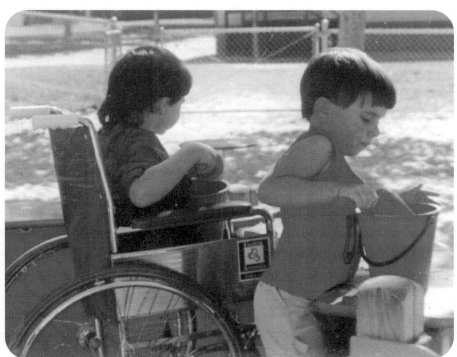

A raised surface allows a child in a wheelchair to participate side by side with peers.

could have a ramp for children who cannot negotiate stairs. Although there is specialized play equipment on the market for children with disabilities, most of it is costly and thus might be impractical to purchase unless your program serves a number of children needing such adaptive equipment.

There are, however, some fairly simple ways to make outdoor play accessible and enjoyable for children with special needs. For example, you could provide the following modifications:

This design safely holds even older, heavier preschoolers.

- A raised sensory table (sand, water, etc.) to accommodate wheelchairs and walkers
- Activity or manipulative panels on the sides of a climbing structure or fence (see Appendix B, p. 89)
- A table or picnic bench for manipulative/creative activities
- A wide doorway to a playhouse
- A paved area underneath a climbing structure for a secret hideout
- Lightweight balls or objects suspended on string (similar to a tetherball)
- Adapted riding toys (available commercially), including a wagon with raised sides
- A swing made from a small tire with part of the side cut away to enable a child to nestle securely inside (see accompanying illustration)

See Appendix B, p. 89, for a detailed list of suggested materials and equipment for children with special needs. This list also provides information on the developmental benefits of these items.

Vegetation[2]

Vegetation can contribute beauty and interest to your outdoor play space. Some vegetation, like hedges, can also provide protection from places outside the playground, such as streets and parking lots. However, special care should be taken when choosing vegetation. Thorny or prickly bushes can cut and scratch children. Some plants are naturally toxic at particular times in their growth cycle, and young children may be attracted to the small buds and berries of these plants. Dermatitis can result from handling toxic plants or plants that have been treated with pesticides.

---

[2]Information in this section adapted from *The Early Childhood Playground: An Outdoor Classroom,* by S. Esbensen, 1987, Ypsilanti, MI: High/Scope Press. Used with permission.

These warnings are not intended to steer you away from landscaping your playground with plants and natural materials. As noted in an earlier chapter, a list of toxic and nontoxic vegetation is provided in Appendix C (see p. 94) to help you choose safe landscaping materials.

Raising Funds for Play Equipment

Although you will naturally want to purchase high-quality equipment, cost considerations may deter you. Keep in mind that you may be able to purchase several smaller items for the same cost as one large "do-everything" structure. If adequate funding is not available, consider purchasing a few items at a time as your budget allows, gradually building a fully furnished playground. Structures such as playhouses; climbers; sandboxes; tire swings; and tables, chairs, or benches may be donated by individuals or community organizations. In my hometown, an old fire engine has been a popular playground fixture for 20 or more years. When it deteriorated to the point of causing injuries to children, the park board repaired it, much to the delight of both children and parents.

When undertaking a project to raise funds for play equipment, it is important to prepare a master plan for the whole project and clearly state your goals. For example, a statement such as "By January of next year, we will have a covered sand pit and sand toys" will keep the project in focus and provide a targeted goal for those involved from the community. Your fundraising project must have a strong commitment from a committee of enthusiastic people.

Consider the following as you plan your fundraising endeavors:

- It is not that much more difficult to raise large amounts of money than small amounts.
- Although most donations are from individual donors, local businesses and service organizations can also serve as resources.
- Your best sources of donations are from those who have donated to you before.

- Givers gauge their donation against other contributors.
- Donors appreciate knowing specifically what their donation will provide, such as a component of a play structure or a shrub.
- Fundraising is selling. Promote your product to appeal to different customers. For example, a local business may be motivated to enhance children's cognitive abilities while a neighborhood association may want to contribute to children's social development.
- Unless they request anonymity, publicly acknowledge donors for their contributions. Corporate donors, in particular, are often motivated by community recognition.
- Don't forget the families your program serves—they are the most interested in seeing that their children have safe, enjoyable playgrounds!

There are two methods of fundraising: direct and indirect solicitation. Direct fundraising involves asking donors for money or having them purchase a specific piece of play equipment for your center. Indirect fundraising activities involve selling items such as cookies or raffle tickets to raise the money for equipment.

When fundraising, choose an articulate and persuasive member of your committee to keep your project in the community's awareness as much as possible through news articles, letters to interested parties, and local media. Do not be discouraged by what seems to be an ambitious goal. Phasing the project, or leasing specific equipment to own, may help you reach your goal.

Civic and national foundations and organizations are potential sources for funding a new playground or updating an old one. Some municipalities also give grants to assist with making playgrounds accessible. Service clubs, such as the Junior League, Jaycees, Kiwanis, and Rotary, often are interested in donating to such projects. Listings of U.S. government funding agencies and grants are available through sources such as the Federal Register and the Foundation Center. You may contact the Foundation Center in Washington, D.C., by calling 202-331-1400.

Summary

In this chapter we have presented a variety of stationary equipment and loose materials for outdoor play and have discussed the issues related to incorporating them into the playground setting. Yet, while making the playground fun and challenging for children is a worthy goal, we also need to make sure the play space is safe. In the next chapter we offer strategies for making playgrounds as safe as possible.

5 Safety

||||||||||||||||||||||||||||||||

Safety is a very real issue for all those who work with young children, indoors or out. Poorly designed playgrounds and equipment can be dangerous, as evidenced by news stories and a number of successful lawsuits in recent years. Consider these facts from the U.S. Consumer Product Safety Commission (1996):

- In the U.S., 148,000 injuries sustained on public playgrounds are treated in emergency rooms annually.
- 60% of these public playground injuries are caused by falls.
- 15 children die each year as a result of playground injuries.

While these statistics are certainly of concern to those involved in setting up and supervising playgrounds, it is helpful to examine them more closely. For instance, when Ball (1995), a British statistician, analyzed the 15 deaths that occurred in one year on U.S. playgrounds, he found that 5 of these occurred in backyards, 5 were due to vehicles hitting children in a playground area, and only 5 actually occurred on or around public play equipment. Although this information does not diminish the seriousness of playground hazards, outdoor play actually carries the same or less risk than other daily activities or routines that children might be engaged in (Ball, 1995). Wallach (1997) makes a distinction between risk and hazard. A *risk* is a challenging opportunity for children to test their strength and ability.

Adults' excessive concerns about children's safety can negatively impact the level of challenge in the outdoor play space.

Although safety is an important consideration outdoors, children should have many opportunities to challenge themselves.

Children are continually engaging in activities that physically and mentally challenge their abilities, and some risk is necessary for their growth and development. A *hazard*, on the other hand, is a dangerous situation that cannot be perceived by children. Children do not know, for example, that their heads could become entrapped between railings if the space is of a certain dimension. They may not notice a protruding bolt or understand that if an overhead beam is rusted, it could collapse when too much weight is swung from it. Greenman (1995, p. 60) expresses the importance of providing a balance between challenge and safety outdoors:

> The drive to protect our children is profound and easily can extend to scotch-guarding their lives. Scrubbing and polishing every raw experience in the name of health and safety or protecting innocence scrapes away the natural luster of childhood. Some of the wonders and joys of childhood that fuel the best in our adult selves are unavoidably birthed in bumps and bruises and tears.

Our responsibility as educators and caregivers is to make informed decisions on playground materials and equipment so that we can minimize the safety hazards to children while providing a challenging play environment. The information contained in this chapter will provide guidelines for doing so.

Playground Safety Factors

The National Program for Playground Safety was established in 1995 to act as a clearinghouse and resource center for communities wanting to make playgrounds safer for children (see Appendix D, p. 97). After analyzing available research, program staff identified the following four critical factors for keeping children safe:

1. **Supervision is adequate.** Adults need to watch for hazards while observing and participating in children's activities.

2. **Equipment is age- and size-appropriate.** Toddlers and preschoolers have different body proportions, skills, and abilities than elementary-aged children. Specific body dimensions for children aged 2–8 are given in Appendix E (see p. 99) to help you ensure that your playground equipment is properly scaled.

3. **Impact-absorbing surfaces are adequate.** As discussed later in this chapter, it is important that the amount of cushioning present is sufficient for the height of the equipment in the event of a fall. Surfaces underneath play equipment should not be made of concrete, asphalt, blacktop, packed earth, grass, or rock.

4. **Equipment is properly maintained.** Equipment should be anchored safely with no exposed concrete footings. Avoid using open S-hooks on chains, and watch for rust, splinters, and protruding nuts and bolts on equipment.

These general guidelines will be expanded upon in the remainder of this chapter and in Chapter 6.

As toddlers and twos enthusiastically develop their climbing skills, they will benefit from equipment with handrails and high safety siding.

Safety Standards and Guidelines

Government and private agencies in both Canada and the United States have developed safety standards for manufacturers and consumers of play equipment. In addition to national standards, each province or state may have supplementary compliance requirements. In addition, many licensing agencies of school facilities issue their own mandatory or voluntary requirements. Before designing and equipping your play space, consult the appropriate national and local standards. The guidelines of four national agencies are discussed below; refer to Appendix D, p. 97, for contact information.

American Society for Testing and Materials

The ASTM Document F1487-98, *Standard Consumer Safety Performance Specification for Playground Equipment for Public Use* (1999), provides national safety standards for playground equipment for children aged 2 through 12. Although this is a voluntary standard, Dr. Fran Wallach, Chair of the ASTM Committee that developed Standard F1487, states that this document is "acceptable in courts, equipment design, and proposals." She also warns that the ultimate decision regarding liability rests with the courts, and playground operators are very vulnerable if they do not comply (personal communication, March 22, 1999).

The International Playground Equipment Manufacturers Association (IPEMA) was formed in 1996 to grant third-party safety certification of play equipment. Equipment that has the IPEMA seal has met an independent testing laboratory's assessment criteria for compliance with ASTM Standard F1487.

U.S. Consumer Product Safety Commission

The CPSC publishes the *Handbook for Public Playground Safety* (1997), which is intended for use by parks and recreation personnel, school officials, and equipment purchasers/installers. It is less technical than the ASTM standard. This commission has also published *Tips for Playground Safety* (1996), a document that explains injuries from public playground-related incidents and gives suggestions for reducing hazards. Dr. Fran Wallach (personal communication, March 22, 1999) summarizes that the ASTM and CPSC standards are now compatible except in two instances: 1) slope of stairway and 2) size of a platform at the top of a slide. Most states require that you meet the criteria outlined in one or the other or both. Wallach also recommends referring to the CPSC guidelines for

WARNING!

Clothing strings, loose clothing, and stringed items placed around the neck can strangle a child. Never dress children in loose or stringed clothing if they will be on playground equipment.

From *Strings Can Strangle Children on Playground Equipment* (Document #5094), by the U.S. Consumer Product Safety Commission. Web site: *www.cpsc.gov/cpscpub/pubs/chld_sfy.html*

surfacing specifics and to the ASTM standards for accessibility requirements.

Canadian Standards Association

The Canadian Standards Association (CSA) recently revised its 1990 standard on playground equipment. It provides guidelines for children aged 18 months through 12 years and covers areas such as surfacing, installation, play-space layout, and specific play equipment. Although the standard is currently voluntary, in most municipalities adherence to it can substantially reduce the risk of liability in the event of an accident.

Members from both the ASTM and CSA committees are studying U.S. and Canadian requirements for manufactured playground equipment. The revised documents created by this joint committee will result in comparable standards for the two countries.

U.S. Access Board

In addition to specific standards for outdoor play equipment, there are federal requirements for playground accessibility. The Architectural and Transportation Barriers Compliance Board, or the Access Board, is an independent, 25-member federal agency responsible for promoting accessibility for individuals with disabilities. This committee is in the process of amending accessibility guidelines mandated by the Americans with Disabilities Act of 1990 (ADA), a comprehensive civil rights law prohibiting discrimination on the basis of disability. It dictates that all newly constructed and renovated government, public, and commercial buildings be accessible by people with disabilities.

The Access Board's new accessibility guidelines for outdoor play areas will cover such issues as the following:

- Separate play areas for 2–5-year-olds and 5–12-year-olds
- Entry and exit points
- Primary and auxiliary pathways
- Ground level and elevated play components
- Activity panels
- Resilient surfacing

The Dirty Dozen: Causes of Playground Injuries

This list of the 12 leading causes of playground injuries was compiled by the National Playground Safety Institute as a guideline for checking play-space safety. For the complete checklist, contact the National Recreation and Park Association. (Web site: *www.nrpa.org/playsafe/dirtyd~1.htm*. See Appendix D, p. 97, for address and telephone information.)

1. *Improper protective surfacing.* Impact-absorbing materials must maintain enough depth and resiliency to cushion potential falls.

2. *Inadequate fall zone.* Impact-absorbing materials should cover the area underneath equipment and 6 feet beyond. This zone should be free of other equipment or obstructions.

3. *Protrusion and entanglement hazards.* Watch for equipment components or protruding hardware that might cut a child or catch on clothing, causing strangulation.

4. *Entrapment in openings.* Openings on rungs and platforms should be less than $3\frac{1}{2}$ inches or greater than 9 inches to avoid entrapment of children's heads.

5. *Insufficient equipment spacing.* Equipment should be at least 12 feet apart; otherwise, play areas become crowded and children may collide with one another or with equipment.

6. *Trip hazards.* Exposed concrete footings, tree roots, rocks, and abrupt changes in elevation can cause children to trip.

7. *Lack of supervision.* Adults need to be alert, able to scan the entire play space, and reach children quickly in the event of an accident.

8. *Age-inappropriate activities.* Use only equipment that is intended for a particular age group. Preschoolers and school-aged children should have separate outdoor play spaces.

9. *Lack of maintenance.* Equipment must be inspected for broken, loose, or deteriorating components, and resilient surfacing should also be maintained.

10. *Pinch, crush, shearing, and sharp-edge hazards.* Moving components that might crush or pinch a child's finger should be eliminated or modified to prevent this hazard. Chain links on swings should be less than $\frac{5}{16}$ inch (8mm) in diameter.

11. *Platforms with no guardrails.* Guardrails should be on all preschool equipment surfaces that are over 20 inches high. Use vertical rails rather than horizontal rails to prevent children from climbing on the railing.

12. *Equipment not recommended for public playgrounds.* This includes metal swings with seats in the shape of animals, merry-go-rounds, and trapeze bars.

- Handrails
- Ramps and wheelchair lifts
- Cost-effectiveness

Safety Surfacing

Surfacing is the foundation of the outdoor play space. There are two categories of surfaces: *functional,* or *play,* and *safety,* or *resilient*—the impact-absorbing materials found beneath play structures.

Functional surfacing will be determined by the kinds of play that will take place in various areas of the playground. For instance, a firm surface such as asphalt, rubber tile, or concrete is necessary for wheeled toys and wheelchair access. A grassy surface invites children to run, chase, and roll. A nature area would need dirt for digging and gardening.

Since approximately 60 percent of all playground injuries are caused by falls to the ground (U.S. Consumer Product Safety Commission, 1996), resilient surfacing is critical to children's safety. There are many different materials available; a description of the most common safety surfaces is given here.

Types of Safety Surfacing

Sand

The size and composition of sand particles determine the sand's quality and function. As mentioned in the previous chapter, safety sand should be loosely packed to yield on impact and cushion children's falls. The best granule size for impact absorption is 2mm–6mm in diameter; most of the particles in the mixture should measure in the middle of this range. Crushed sand contains powder residue that packs the sand and decreases its shock absorbency.

Pea gravel

This material consists of large pea-shaped stones. It has about the same shock absorbency as sand and is often available for a fraction of the cost of river-washed sand. To be most effective in absorbing

Safety surfacing is critical for cushioning the inevitable tumbles children experience during their outdoor explorations.

Like shoes on a person's feet or tires on a car, surfacing materials can simply be functional or an integral part of the overall design.

impacts, the stones should be rounded and of uniform size, with no exposed shards. Bird's-eye pea stones do not track into buildings (as sand can), but they are potential hazards because they can be thrown and ingested.

Engineered wood fibers

This material, which consists of elongated hardwood fibers with no bark or leaves, differs from bark mulch or chips that contain chipped limbs, bark, twigs, and branches. Make sure that no preservatives have been used that are toxic or could cause skin allergies in children. Cedar-based chips can also cause problems for children with skin sensitivities.

Rubber matting

One of the most expensive surfaces, this material is made from recycled rubber particles bonded together with an adhesive. Rubber tiles are molded using vulcanized virgin or recycled rubber; poured-in-place systems are usually composed of a recycled rubber base coat and a colored virgin rubber top coat. Some rubber matting requires a firm base underneath it, such as concrete.

For a comparison of these safety surfaces, see the table on the opposite page.

Choosing Safety Surfacing Materials

There are four primary factors to consider when choosing resilient surfacing: **shock absorbency, accessibility, maintenance,** and **cost** (Henderson, 1997).

Shock absorbency

Materials vary greatly in resiliency—the amount they will yield upon impact. Shock absorbency depends not only on the resiliency of the material but also on its depth; the less resilient a material,

Comparison of Playground Surfacing Materials

MATERIALS	ADVANTAGES	DISADVANTAGES
Loose Organic Materials— Wood Chips, Bark Mulch, Engineered Wood Fibers	Low initial cost Easy to install Less attractive to pets Readily available Engineered wood fiber may be accessible	Subject to environmental conditions Decomposes Subject to fungus Easily displaced Requires containment borders Requires good drainage Continuous maintenance
Loose Inorganic Materials— Sand, Gravel	Low initial cost Easy to install Nonflammable Readily available	May be affected by environmental conditions Combines with dirt or may compact Not accessible Abrasive to floors, skin Conceals animal excrement and debris Easily displaced Continuous maintenance Requires containment borders
Loose Synthetic Materials— Chopped Rubber, Plastics	Easy to install Slow to decompose Not subject to fungus growth Nonabrasive Readily available Does not deteriorate Less likely to compact	Higher initial cost Flammable May contain contaminants from processing Not accessible Easily displaced Continuous maintenance Requires containment borders Requires good drainage
Fixed Synthetic Materials— Rubber Tiles, Poured-in-Place Rubber/Urethane Combinations	Easy to clean Consistent shock absorbency— does not compact Not attractive to pets Optional colors available Minimal maintenance Generally accessible Not displaced Generally does not require containment border Some materials can be installed over concrete, asphalt, stone	High initial cost May be susceptible to frost damage May be flammable Requires skilled installation Subject to vandalism Often must be used on level surfaces

Note: Adapted from *Handbook for Public Playground Safety* (Document #325), by the U.S. Consumer Product Safety Commission, 1997. Web site: *www.cpsc.gov/cpscpub/pubs/chld_sfty.html*

the greater the depth necessary to provide adequate cushioning. Some of the most resilient surfaces are wood chips, sand, and pea gravel. Rubber matting is also effective. Some materials, including packed earth, concrete, and asphalt, have no "give" and thus are not effective safety surfaces at any depth.

Critical height describes the maximum height from which a child could be expected to fall without receiving a life-threatening head injury (U.S. Consumer Product Safety Commission, 1996). Any material used must be deep enough to provide sufficient absorbency relative to the height of the equipment above it. It is recommended that loose-fill materials—sand, gravel, wood chips—be at least 12 inches deep (U.S. Consumer Product Safety Commission, 1997). See the table to the left for a comparison chart of the critical heights for safety surfaces mentioned in this chapter.

Fall Height (in Feet) From Which a Life-Threatening Head Injury Would Not Be Expected

COMMON LOOSE-FILL MATERIALS	6" depth	9" depth	12" depth
Fine Sand	5	5	9
Coarse Sand	5	5	6
Fine Gravel	6	7	10
Medium Gravel	5	5	6
Wood Chips (Engineered Wood Fibers)	6	7	12

Shock absorbency information for rubber products can be obtained from manufacturers.

Note: Adapted from *Handbook for Public Playground Safety* (Doc. #325, 1997) and *Tips for Public Playground Safety* (Doc. #324, 1996), by the U.S. Consumer Product Safety Commission. Web site: *www.cpsc.gov/cpscpub/pubs/chld_sfty.html*

Accessibility

The only resilient surfacing that is currently considered fully accessible and impact absorbing is rubber matting; engineered wood fiber is also generally accessible. However, since equipping an entire playground with either of these materials could limit play value and be cost prohibitive for programs, the Access Board recommends having accessible surfaces underneath equipment that children with assistive devices will be able to use independently, and loose-fill materials underneath other types of structures. Children may need adult assistance to use equipment that has nonaccessible safety surfacing. The paths between play structures should be covered with accessible material to allow children to get to them independently.

Maintenance

Loose-fill materials require the most upkeep because they collect debris, scatter easily, and over time become packed down. You should rake and inspect these materials weekly, and add to or replace them every 1–3 years. Manufactured rubber matting requires far less regular maintenance but may become damaged due to extreme temperatures or vandalism.

Cost

Loose-fill materials, particularly sand and pea gravel, are usually the least expensive surfaces initially but may, as mentioned above, require more maintenance. The following list (Henderson, 1997) shows the relative initial costs of common playground surfaces from the least expensive to the most expensive:

To help keep maintenance simple, separate safety surfacing with borders such as railroad ties.

- Gravel
- Sand
- Wood chips
- Rubber tile
- Troweled-in-place rubber

Summary

As this chapter explains, there are many safety factors to consider when setting up your playground. Be sure that all purchased and donated equipment conforms to any standards in your area. Also, carefully compare available safety surfaces in terms of ease of maintenance, shock absorbency, accessibility, and cost. Following the guidelines presented in this chapter will help you to choose equipment and resilient surfaces that will allow children to safely explore the outdoor play area. Use the General Maintenance Checklist and Inspection Forms (see Appendix F, p. 101) to assess the condition of your playground site and equipment.

The adult's role does not end with ensuring that the playground is physically safe. The next chapter will explore ways in which adults help children learn from and enjoy their outdoor experiences.

6 Supporting Children's Outdoor Play: The Adult's Role

In an increasingly litigious society, the role of adults in "policing" playgrounds has been encouraged, but this is not the role they should play. Instead, teachers and caregivers should continue to support and encourage children during outdoor play just as they do during indoor time. Because of the important supportive role adults assume in children's outdoor play, it is essential that the playground be designed to accommodate their need to participate in activities at the child's level. Adults also need to be able to see all parts of the playground at once to facilitate their child observations. Thus, a playground must not only be child-friendly but also adult-friendly. The outdoor play space should enable adults to safely observe and playfully interact with the children in their care so that they can fully capture naturally occurring teachable moments as they happen. Young children's outside play is not a time for adults to relax. On the early childhood playground, adults should look for opportunities to participate in children's play, including offering materials to enhance and extend the play, helping children discover answers to their questions, and assisting children in finding solutions to their problems. Adult assistance, modeling, and support are offered rather than instruction

> Children learn through play by interaction with objects and socialization with peers and with supportive adults.
>
> **FROST, 1997, p. 60**

and control (Frost, 1996). Hohmann and Weikart (1995) make this observation concerning the adult's role during outdoor play: "[Adults] focus all their attention on children to understand and support children's outdoor initiatives in a playful, nonmanagerial way" (p. 285).

Strategies for Adults

Following are some specific strategies that adults can use to appropriately support children's outdoor explorations and ensure playground safety (see also Hohmann & Weikart, 1995, pp. 285–288).

Encourage Children to Think About Their Activities

Adults can assist children in planning their outdoor activities simply by asking them, before or during outdoor time, what they would like to do. Start by commenting on their interests and recent activities and perhaps making a suggestion: "Shawn, yesterday you seemed to enjoy looking at the bird's nest. Would you like to look at it again today and see if anything has happened to the eggs?" Doing this not only communicates your interest in and respect for children's ideas but also helps children think about and clarify their intentions.

Observe and Note Children's Interests and Activities

Being involved with children outdoors offers an excellent opportunity for adults to learn more about their thoughts, interests, and skills. How do children interact with other children? With other adults? Which children are playing alone? Why? How do children move on the playground—what is their movement pattern? What can I add to the play space to support and extend the children's activities? By answering these and similar questions, through your careful observations, you can plan for and build on children's individual interests and abilities, as in the example about the bird's nest, above. Observing children while they play will also help you identify children who may need extra support or encouragement to try new challenges, vary their activities, or interact with other children.

Having children verbalize their plans encourages continuity between thought and action and communicates respect for their play.

Bodrova & Leong (1996)

Provide a Variety of Toys and Materials

In the previous chapter we recommended that loose manipulative materials be brought onto the playground each day and stored away when not in use (balls, riding toys, art materials, role-play items, and so on). By offering these materials in addition to the permanent structures on the playground, children have a rich variety of props and objects to inspire and support their play. Vary the materials, particularly as children's interest wanes or turns to new pursuits. For instance, if you overhear children discussing their experiences at a car wash, you could provide buckets of water, cloths, and wheeled toys for a "car wash" on the playground. Making meaningful links between indoor and outdoor settings can extend children's play and enhance their understanding of the world around them. Bring dress-up clothes and instruments outside for a child-directed performance, or have paper and markers available to make nature tracings after children have done a similar activity with indoor objects.

For a change of pace, hold your group time outdoors!

Participate Actively in Children's Play and Conversations When Appropriate

Participating in children's outdoor activities when children are willing to include us allows adults to support children's outdoor choices and

Write a story with children about the role-playing you observe them engaging in outdoors—they will love starring in it!

Children's experiences outside of school can spark new ideas for outdoor play. Teachers added this tent to their playground after hearing children discuss family camping trips.

Provide outdoor equipment and activities that invite adults to play with children—a group spring toy with enough room for an adult, or a comfortable spot in the sandbox.

enhance their physical, social, and cognitive development. Teachers and caregivers actively participate in children's play by

- **Joining in children's activities on their level:** Rather than leading or directing children's play, follow their lead and join in their activities as a partner. Jump in a leaf pile, throw a ball back and forth, play tag, or together watch a blade of grass float towards the drain. Look for opportunities to join children as they observe, experiment with, and draw conclusions about nature and the world around them. Following a child's lead does not mean that you cannot suggest new ideas to extend children's play. If children are stumped for a prop idea, for instance, give them a suggestion—then let *them* decide whether to accept or decline your suggestion.

When participating in children's play, adults follow the children's lead.

- **Conversing with children:** Outside play offers rich opportunities to talk with children. Conversations often occur during repetitive activities such as swinging or digging in the sand. Verbally describe children's actions: "I see a big tower of sand here!" Then, respond to children's conversational leads, commenting and expanding on the statements they make. This allows children to keep control of the conversation while giving you some insight into their thoughts and the topics that are important to them. Ask questions sparingly; focus instead on exploring with the children the answers to their own questions.

• **Encouraging children to problem solve:** As children play outside, they encounter all kinds of problems to solve. The squirrels have eaten all the birdseed from the bird feeder, the swings have large puddles underneath, or the cardboard fort is flattened from children crashing into it. Encourage children to brainstorm solutions to their problems, giving only as much support as necessary. Children will often come up with creative solutions on their own with appropriate adult support and encouragement.

Assist Children in Resolving Conflicts

When conflicts arise on the playground, suggest that children take responsibility for solving the problems themselves. This gives them a greater sense of control over the situation and encourages them to work together. Listen matter-of-factly to what children say about the issue, describing what you understand the problem to be: "You both want to ride that bike." Ask for their ideas on what to do, and help them consider their suggestions until a solu-

Steps in Resolving Conflicts*

1. *Approach calmly, stopping any hurtful actions.*
   • **Place yourself between the children, on their level.**
   • **Use a calm voice and gentle touch.**
   • **Remain neutral rather than take sides.**
2. *Acknowledge children's feelings.*
   • **"You look really upset."**
   • **Let children know you need to hold any object in question.**
3. *Gather information.*
   • **"What's the problem?"**
4. *Restate the problem.*
   • **"So the problem is. . ."**
5. *Ask for ideas for solutions and choose one together.*
   • **"What can we do to solve this problem?"**
   • **Encourage children to think of a solution.**
6. *Be prepared to give follow-up support.*
   • **"You solved the problem!"**
   • **Stay near the children.**

© 1998 High/Scope Educational Research Foundation
*Taken from *Supporting Children in Resolving Conflicts* (24-minute color video). Ypsilanti, MI: High/Scope Press, 1998. Used with permission.

Taking a problem-solving approach to conflicts enables children to develop the skills they need to handle situations themselves.

tion is agreed upon. The six-step process for resolving conflicts presented on the opposite page is a well-tested set of guidelines for adults to use in conflict situations. It is effective in resolving disputes and in enabling children to suggest strategies and solutions.

Watch for Dangerous Situations

It is estimated that 40 percent of playground accidents are due to inadequate adult supervision (U.S. Consumer Product Safety Commission, 1997). Setting limits and having simple, clear rules for children to follow when playing outside will help prevent many hazardous situations; however, adults always need to be alert for unsafe situations as children play. Careful observation and being actively engaged in children's activities enable adults to be close by so that they can spot and prevent dangers more quickly. Avoid becoming so involved with one child or one group of children, however, that you cannot maintain a view of all the children on the playground. You must be able to scan the entire area and be able to reach children quickly when necessary. Young children enjoy hiding in nooks and crannies outside; avoid having places that adults cannot reach in emergencies. See the box at right for further supervision recommendations.

As mentioned earlier, concern for children's safety outdoors sometimes leads to unnecessary restrictions on their activities. Remember that children need to challenge themselves both physically and mentally. With properly func-

Supervision

The National Program for Playground Safety (see Appendix D, p. 97) has recommended steps that can ensure adequate adult supervision of the play space:

a. *Maintain an adequate ratio of adults to children.* There should be no difference between the ratio inside and outside. Adult supervision should be related to the kind of activity occurring.

b. *Determine a consistent strategy on how to resolve conflicts.* The outdoor play space is a key arena for modeling and teaching problem-solving skills. Avoid solving problems for children. Instead, assist them in finding solutions and resolving conflicts for themselves.

c. *Learn the basics of playground equipment safety and inspection.* Supervisors do not need to be certified safety inspectors but a rudimentary understanding of maintenance will be helpful. They should make daily visual inspections of the equipment and have at least a basic familiarity with the common causes of playground injuries (see p. 60).

d. *Establish a plan for when accidents do occur.* Basic first aid equipment and phone numbers of emergency personnel and parents or guardians should be readily accessible. Use an incident report form (see Appendix G, p. 116) to document playground injuries.

tioning equipment, a well-designed play space, and observant, involved adults, children will be able to safely and confidently try out new limits for themselves. Such a play space will require only a few rules that children must follow. Guidelines for setting rules are presented at left.

Provide Sufficient Time for Play and Cleanup

Adults sometimes cut short the amount of time children stay outdoors because they are concerned that a long play period will cause children to become bored and aimless in their play. By providing a number of interesting and appropriate materials and activities on the playground, however, you will ensure that children have enough choices to keep them actively involved in play. Allow children sufficient time to explore, play creatively, and exercise their bodies. Give children a few minutes' warning before outside time is over so that they can bring some closure to their play and assist with cleanup. An easy storage and retrieval system for loose manipulatives will help make cleanup go more smoothly.

Summary

As in the indoor learning environment, outdoor play offers teachers and caregivers valuable opportunities to both interact with and observe children. When adults are actively involved in children's playground experiences, they can support children in their choices, expand their play through the provision of extra materials and appropriate suggestions, participate as partners in play, assist in problem solving and conflict resolution, and ensure that children explore the outdoors safely. When playground

---

Guidelines for Setting Rules for the Playground

Establish only a few rules and then enforce them consistently. When deciding which rules to adopt, ask yourself the following questions: What am I trying to accomplish with this rule? What is the probability of a serious debilitating injury arising from not following the rule? Are the children in my care developmentally ready for such a limit? Is there a problem in layout, equipment, routine, or design that, when corrected, will eliminate the need for this rule?

1. Keep the number of rules to a minimum.

2. Involve children in rule making as much as possible: "Some children have gotten hurt this week jumping off the climber. What do you think we can do to stop having children get hurt?" Being part of the decision making encourages children to feel more responsible for keeping a rule.

3. State each rule clearly in a positive way and give a simple reason for it: "Go down the slide after the person in front of you gets off so that no one gets hurt." Children more readily comply with a rule if they can understand the reason for it.

4. Demonstrate the behavior you *do* want.

5. Enforce limits consistently.

Adapted from the National Program for Playground Safety. Web site: *www.uni.edu/playground/*

Joining in outdoor play gives adults a chance to learn more about children's skills and interests.

design ensures that adults can easily interact with and carefully observe children by stepping back and scanning the entire play area, they can quickly identify safety issues and also identify children's interests and developmental levels just as they do during other parts of the day in other areas of the learning environment.

7 Playground Assessment Case Study

You should now have a preliminary understanding of the way to approach the design or renovation of your outdoor play space. The criteria outlined in the previous chapters and in the appendices can be applied to a variety of private and public playgrounds. To illustrate how to proceed with renovating an existing outdoor play space, we have provided the following example.

The playground observed for this case study belongs to a preschool in the Pacific Northwest. This preschool, located in a house, operates year round and enrolls 25 children per session. The children are between 3 and 5 years old, with some 6-year-olds enrolled in the summer program. Most are at the preoperational stage of cognitive development and engage in parallel, associative, and cooperative social play. There is an open in-out policy for the playground, allowing children to go outdoors whenever they wish during the daily routine.

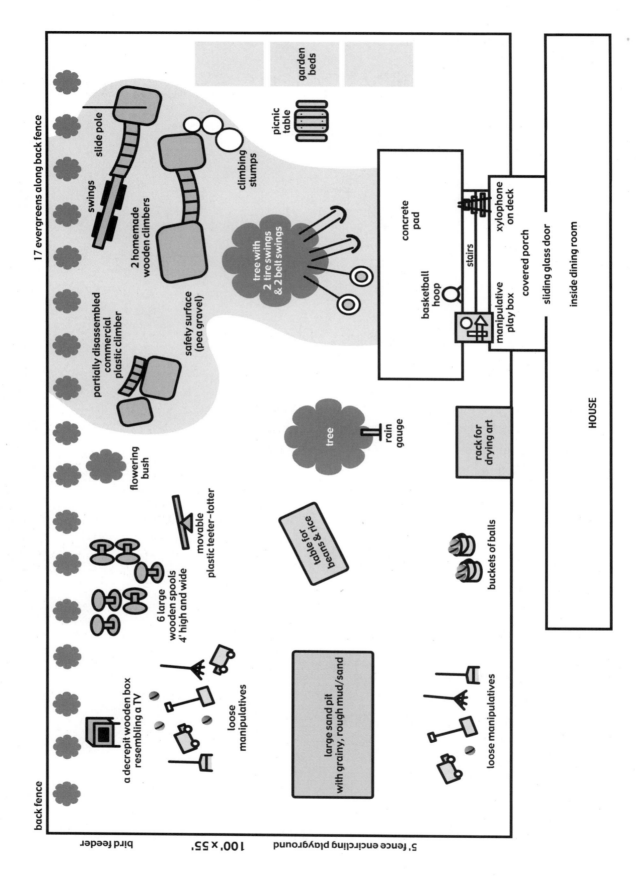

Case Study: A Playground Needing Renovation

Physical Characteristics of the Playground

The first impression when viewing this playground (depicted on the facing page) is the size of the yard and the beauty of the trees. The site measures 55 feet by 100 feet. There are 17 evergreen trees bordering the playground and 2 mature trees in the center of the space. One of these trees has strong limbs and supports 2 tire swings and 2 belt swings. There is a new, 5-foot-tall cedar fence surrounding the entire space. The playground is well protected from strong winds because of its position on the street and proximity to the house and trees. Although the terrain is flat, there is some puddling, indicating that drainage might be a problem during the winter's worst downpours. There is a water outlet and hose beside the house.

The Surrounding Community

The center is in a somewhat undeveloped part of the city, with a large field on one side. The area has three main public playgrounds where children play. The community surrounding this preschool is predominately middle class. Because this preschool is not a full-day program and most of the children have a stay-at-home parent, the children may have fewer chances to socialize with other children and to engage in challenging physical play. Thus, this center's playground serves an important function in the lives of the children there.

Reflecting Program Values

The values of this program are reflected in the children's artwork freely displayed indoors, the sights and sounds of active outdoor play, and signs reminding adults that

- Children don't need to be treated equally; they need to be treated uniquely.
- Every voice counts.
- If it hasn't been in the hand, it can't be in the brain.
- Children don't need all things taught to them; they need a means to teach themselves.

The teachers in this program have identified their top three objectives for the outdoor play space as (1) providing children with experiences with nature; (2) providing children with a place to run and play freely; and (3) providing children with opportunities to socialize with their peers in an outdoor setting. Teachers view their role as that of providing an active learning setting, and they show a great deal of respect for the children's ability to handle conflicts themselves. Although the center's open in-out policy for the playground allows children more choices during the day, it also sometimes leaves children outside without direct supervision. This is a definite safety hazard and should be corrected immediately by ensuring that an adult is responsibly supervising children on the playground at all times. This may require a change in the routine that would establish definite times for outdoor play and adequate adult supervision.

General Characteristics of the Playground

The middle third of the playground is covered with worn-looking pea gravel. The playground is entered from sliding glass doors that open onto a small covered porch. The porch has a manipulative play box off to the left and a xylophone attached to the stair railing. Although this is a nice transition area, children must walk down the stairs and pass through the area where a basketball hoop is located in order to get onto the playground. This could create space conflicts and could be hazardous to those entering the playground. To the right of the porch is a focal/social zone with three garden beds and a comfortable wooden table with seating for six.

Near the back fence are three medium-sized climbing structures. The two wooden ones are clearly homemade. The third one, a plastic manufactured structure that has been partially disassembled, presents a risk for children expecting sturdiness when they climb it. Both of the homemade structures are scaled to fit young children, offer several activities appropriate for the ages of the children, and have plenty of access and egress points. There are some major concerns with these structures, however. First, they are old and their paint is peeling off. Second, the unique three-stump system of access is located within the fall zone of the structure, and the final stump is only 8 inches from a slide pole. These conditions could cause a space conflict or serious injury in the case of a fall. A third concern is the proximity of the swing set to the climber and to a nearby tree. Because of its low height (about 6 feet), it is quite likely that children can get to the top of the swing beam. This in itself is a hazard, and another concern is that there are exposed bolts on the top of the swing set. The protrusions are almost an inch long and could cause harm if a child fell on them or if they caught on a piece of clothing.

Along the back fence are six large (4 feet by 4 feet) wooden spools placed in a variety of positions. Their size and arrangement offer possibilities for creative games and role playing, and the children enjoy running around and through the maze of spools. However, because the spools are only 4 feet from the fence, children could fall or jump onto the fence. This hazard could easily be eliminated by moving the spools farther away from the fence.

There is a large sandbox to the left of the porch, filled with a coarse, almost muddy, kind of sand. There are plenty of loose materials nearby, including trucks, pails, and shovels. There is even a board mounted with hangers showing outlines of the shovels so that children can return them by themselves. Although this board doesn't appear to be used much, it offers a good matching activity. There are two large buckets with balls of various types and sizes as well as rakes and brooms.

Playground Accessibility

Children and adults with any kind of motor impairment or assistive device would find it difficult to access this playground. However, because of the amount of space and the flat terrain, making this setting more accessible should be relatively simple and inexpensive. At present, children have to go down a flight of stairs to enter the playground from the main building, so a ramp or some other means of access is necessary for children with special needs. Paved pathways around the play space and between structures would enhance the design for all children but particularly for those using mobility aids.

These pathways would also help define play zones, improving the organization of the play yard. The grassy area, though not fully accessible, is at least uncluttered and allows for plenty of ball play, games, conversations, and teacher-facilitated activities. The basketball hoop needs to be moved out of the way of foot traffic, but the height of the hoop could be changed to accommodate a seated child. Other accommodations, noted in the next section, will improve the outdoor play opportunities for all children.

Recommendations

Several changes to this playground will enhance children's enjoyment and learning outdoors:

- A consistent daily routine with time allocated for outdoor play would assure that adults are always in attendance on the playground.

- As mentioned earlier, creating paved pathways to weave through the site will increase accessibility and facilitate the use of wheeled toys. It will also help define play zones, assisting children in organizing and planning their play activities.

- Due to the safety and location problems with the swing set mentioned earlier, the swings attached to the homemade structure need to be removed. They could be replaced with a separate swing set or with a few spring toys. A spring-based group seesaw would be a nice addition for social play.

- The stump access to the climber should be replaced with a vertical ladder that will not interfere with children playing on the slide pole or on the structure. The stumps themselves can be moved to another area of the playground or used as seating in the garden zone.

- The homemade climbing structures are exhibiting signs of age and use and are unattractive. For now, they should be sanded down and repainted; for long-term planning, the center should begin to save funds to replace the two home-made structures with a new IPEMA-certified one or have new ones donated by parents or members of the community. The commercial climber is also a hazard and should likewise be replaced.

- Staff members could consider raising the garden beds to waist level. This might promote more interaction between adults and children in the garden area and would allow children with mobility devices to comfortably participate in the gardening activities.

- The play sand needs to be replaced with fresh river-washed sand to fully promote sensory and creative play. A seat with a backrest, or a raised play table inside the sand pit, would assist children who may not be able to sit unsupported.

- More opportunities for creative play on this playground would offer additional outdoor choices for children. With Plexiglas and paint trays attached to the fence, it could serve as a large canvas. A second picnic table at the other end of the yard from the existing one would facilitate more adult-supported nature and science activities, such as studying worms and making leaf tracings.

- A focal point or "village well" could be created to give the play space a visual identity for the children. Jay Beckwith, a well-known playground and equipment designer, suggests using a homemade totem pole as a focal point (personal communication, October 1998). Other aids to fostering a sense of community could include establishing a storytelling circle or a set of easels inside one of the pathways. A picnic table with a large, colorful umbrella on it could also serve as a central location where staff and children could gather for snack, conversation, and sharing of discoveries.

- The playground's size makes it difficult to supervise adequately or to provide focus to children's play. Separating play areas by using pathways, shrubs, or a variety of safety surfaces would help make the space more manageable. In addition, a more organized storage space or set of storage cabinets would reduce clutter, allow materials to be used more fully, and encourage children to participate in cleanup.

In conclusion, a center's values are clearly reflected in the way it designs its outdoor play space. In the case study examined here, it is clear that this center encourages interaction with nature, although social interaction seems to be somewhat curtailed due to the size and accessibility of the space and equipment and the lack of identifiable gathering places. With careful planning and possibly a fundraising project, the staff of this center could transform their outdoor site into an exciting, play-rich setting. To do this, staff should establish their priorities for renovation, determine costs, and make a plan for completing each step of the project.

Appendix A
Qualitative Playground Observation Record

Before designing or updating your playground, observe the children playing outdoors to gain an overview of their play patterns and to get a sense of how well the environment supports your program's goals (if you do not yet have a playground, observe another center's). Make notes of the interactions you observe among the children, the environment, and equipment. Your observations should yield the following types of information.

Background Information—
  Date and time of observation:

  Number and age range of children using the play area:

  Climate information:

General observations—

Source: Theemes, T. (1999). *Let's Go Outside! Designing the Early Childhood Playground.* Ypsilanti, MI: High/Scope Press.

Draw a rough bubble diagram of the space, including existing equipment and natural elements.

Is there a balance among creative, social, cognitive, and physical activities? What are children doing with their hands? Their feet? Their whole bodies? How are their minds being challenged by their outdoor activities?

What is the level of noise made by the children outside? What tone of voice do the adults use with children?

Source: Theemes, T. (1999). *Let's Go Outside! Designing the Early Childhood Playground.* Ypsilanti, MI: High/Scope Press.

How active are children in the setting? Are they running, walking, sitting, riding? Are they moving randomly from one area to the next, or are they staying engaged with one activity for longer periods of time?

Social play behavior—record instances of the following social play situations.
   Children playing alone:

   Children playing in pairs:

   Children playing in groups:

Which structures or activities seem to encourage conversations among the children?

Source: Theemes, T. (1999). *Let's Go Outside! Designing the Early Childhood Playground.* Ypsilanti, MI: High/Scope Press.

Write down some of the conversations you hear—
   Between children:

   Between adults and children:

How are the adults spending their time?

In your view, what aspects of the playground seem to best support young children's development?

What materials, activities, natural elements, or other outdoor aspects would you like improved?

Source: Theemes, T. (1999). *Let's Go Outside! Designing the Early Childhood Playground.* Ypsilanti, MI: High/Scope Press.

Appendix B
Common Outdoor Equipment and Materials: Developmental Benefits and Modifications for Children With Special Needs

PLAYGROUND EQUIPMENT

Equipment	Description	Benefits	S	P	E	C*	Modifications for Integrated Play
Play and work tables	Plain or with textured surfaces.	Allow room for quiet individual or group activities. Facilitate adult-child interaction.	X	X	X	X	Backrests on benches for extra support. Room for wheelchair at table height.
Sand table	A container for sand mounted at table height.	Provides sensory stimulation. Encourages language, imagination, problem solving, and creative individual or group play.	X	X	X	X	Room for wheelchair at table height. Indentations around table will enable children with poor balance to lean on table for support.
Play counter	A countertop mounted under a platform or at the side of a ramp or playhouse. May be part of a play sink or stove top.	Encourages role play, imagination, and social interaction. Can also be used for drawing or as a ledge to play with other toys.	X	X	X	X	Appropriate height for wheelchair.
Playhouse	Child-sized house or other enclosed space. Adults should be able to see into it.	Encourages dramatic play and social interaction. Allows children to act out different roles in a safe, supportive atmosphere.	X		X	X	Accessible and large enough to accommodate a child in a wheelchair and peers.
Steering wheel	Mounted on a post, side of wall, or play equipment.	Promotes imaginative play.		X		X	Mounted at wheelchair height. Sounds added so that children with visual impairments can locate.
Tunnel	Plastic molded passageway for crawling through and hiding in.	Challenges children to move their bodies in a different way.		X			Ceiling or side-mounted grips for children to pull their bodies along.

*S = Social   P = Physical   E = Emotional   C = Cognitive

Equipment	Description	Benefits	S	P	E	C*	Modifications for Integrated Play
Wide slide	Double the usual width so that a child can slide down along-side another person.	Encourages socialization and cooperation.	X	X			Accessible for child in wheelchair, with space to transfer from wheel-chair to slide.
Tire swing	Tire used as seat, suspended from beam at a single point. Can seat one or more children.	Improves balance, stimulates vestibular sense, and promotes language and cooperative play.	X	X		X	No modifications needed.
Spring-based seesaw	Seesaw supported by spring rather than fulcrum. Allows children of different sizes to ride together.	Can be used by one or more children; promotes social skills. Strengthens upper body and balance.	X	X	X		Seats made of a nonslip surface will assist with transfer from wheel-chair.
Spring toys	Single-seated rides made in animal or vehicle shapes, mounted on a sturdy coil spring.	Promote upper-body strength and balance; stimulate vestibular sense. Offer place for observation and relaxation/quieting down.		X	X		Back supports and adequate foot holds to provide support. Accessible seating area for transfer out of wheelchair.
Swing	Soft strap or harness seat supported at two points to overhead beam.	Stimulates vestibular sense and promotes balance and coordination. Individual or group play activity.		X	X		Sound-locating device will cue location and timing of swing for safety of children with visual impairments.
Balance beams/pods	Narrow wooden beams or small pod-shaped platforms raised slightly off ground for walking on.	Promote balance, coordination, and gross-motor planning skills. Can be used as a prop for games or as part of obstacle courses.		X		X	Nonslip surface or rail-ings to help children with poor balance.
Manipulative play panel	A counter or panel where knobs, gears, binoculars, dials, or a tick-tack-toe board are mounted.	Improves fine-motor skills and can be cognitively challenging.		X		X	Mounted at different heights to ensure wheelchair access. Add auditory activities and contrasting colors.
Overhead ladder	Horizontal overhead bars at heights appropriate for age and size of children.	Improves gross-motor plan-ning, coordination, and upper-body development.		X		X	Accessible from wheelchair.

* S = Social   P = Physical   E = Emotional   C = Cognitive

Equipment	Description	Benefits	S	P	E	C*	Modifications for Integrated Play
Basketball hoop	Adjustable plastic or steel hoop and frame.	Improves eye-hand coordination and upper-body strength.	X	X		X	Adjustable height allows younger or seated children to play. Movable frame allows for placement in different areas.
Chinning bars	Can be horizontal or inclined. Most appropriate for elementary-aged children.	Improve upper-body development.		X			Mounted at different heights.
Nets	Can be made of cargo chain, rope, or tires. Constructed between platforms or as access devices to climbers.	Challenge balance, eye-hand coordination, and gross-motor planning skills. Strengthen both lower and upper body.	X	X	X	X	Alternate ways to access.
Tube and half tube slides	Enclosed slide allowing children to slide independently. May frighten very young children.	Provide vestibular stimulation.		X	X		Different ways to access.
Stairs	Access to slides, climbers, or platforms; best if wide enough for two children to go up and down simultaneously.	Improve gross-motor planning and lower-body development.		X		X	Bilateral-support railings for young children and those in need of support.
Ladders	Provide access to climbers or platforms. May be inclined or straight.	Improve eye-hand coordination, upper- and lower-body strength, and motor-planning skills. Straight vertical ladder requires more advanced skills.		X		X	Wide enough to permit children to pass each other. Ramped access as alternative.
Bridge	Constructed of wood, tires, rope, or chain. Connects platforms or parts of play equipment. Can be stable or move with child's movements.	Challenges balance and coordination. Can be incorporated into dramatic play activities.		X		X	Handrails for safety. Visual and auditory cues for spatial orientation. Wheelchair accessible and usable.
Talking tubes	Metal or plastic cone-shaped receptacles that transmit sound. Mounted on posts or within a structure.	Promote language and social interaction.	X		X	X	Adjustable mouthpiece for accessibility at different heights.

* S = Social   P = Physical   E = Emotional   C = Cognitive

Equipment	Description	Benefits	S	P	E	C*	Modifications for Integrated Play
Music instruments	Wind chimes, percussion instruments, bell sounded by hand or with a stick.	Improve auditory discrimination skills and encourage creative expression. Can promote group interaction.	X	X	X	X	Placed on appropriate surface and at accessible heights.
Water play table	Water and appropriate toys in bucket; open-container table; or set of sieves, pulleys, and bowls.	Calming for many children. Encourages problem solving, language, tactile awareness, and imaginative play.	X	X	X	X	Indentations around table to accommodate wheelchairs and assist children with poor balance.

PLAYGROUND MATERIALS

Material	Description	Benefits	S	P	E	C*	Comments
Tricycles and other riding toys	Wheeled toys propelled by children's feet or hands. May or may not have pedals.	Foster bilateral coordination, gross-motor skills, and a sense of independence.	X	X	X	X	Need a smooth path made of concrete, rubber tiles, or asphalt. Should be wide enough for two vehicles. Locate away from high-traffic areas.
Push and pull toys	Any toy on wheels that is pulled or pushed, such as wagons, strollers, or carts.	Promote role play, social interaction, language, and balance and coordination.	X	X	X	X	Best on smooth surfaces away from other play areas.
Painting easel	Movable easel on frame or an acrylic sheet attached to a post or fence.	Encourages creative self-expression and promotes fine-motor skills. Can be therapeutic.		X	X	X	Place in a quiet or transitional zone. Variation: have children "paint" the side of a building or fence with a brush and water.
Buckets and shovels	Digging instruments and containers.	Complement sensory play, such as sand, dirt, or mud. Help improve fine-motor skills and eye-hand coordination. Used in solitary or group activities.	X	X	X	X	Pits, piles, or containers of dirt or sand are an essential element of outdoor play.
Spades and trowels	Various gardening tools.	Encourage use of tools. Help develop understanding of and appreciation for nature.	X	X	X	X	Use "real" tools as much as possible.

S = Social   P = Physical   E = Emotional   C = Cognitive

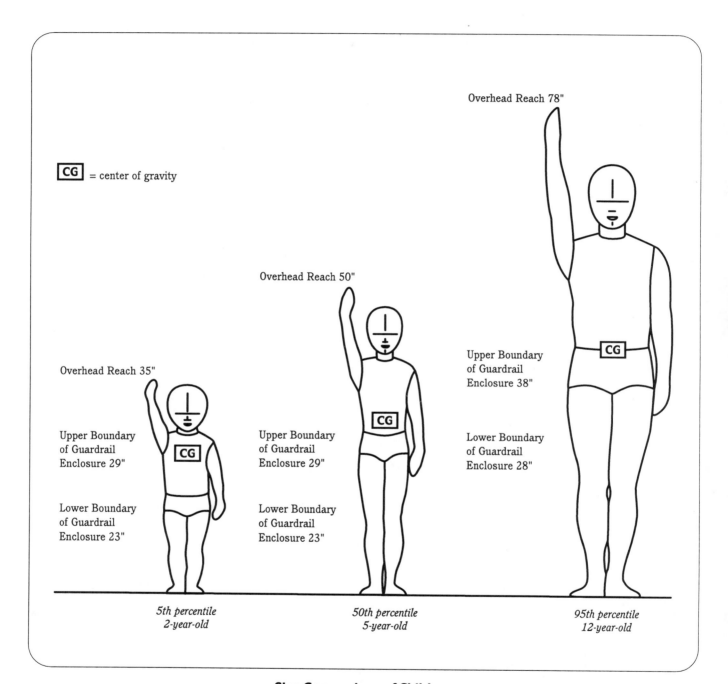

Size Comparison of Children

©NPSI. 1999. Note: Adapted from National Playground Safety Institute Certification Curriculum, National Recreation and Park Association, 1999, Ashburn, VA: NRPA. Used with permission.

Material	Description	Benefits	S	P	E	C*	Comments
Measuring cups and spoons	Any type of measuring instrument.	Promote understanding of comparative size and volume. Assist in development of fine-motor skills.	X	X	X	X	Use in water, sand, dirt, and other sensory materials.
Blocks	Large blocks of any type, homemade or purchased, or manageable planks that children can use to make "forts."	Construction materials promote social play, language, and problem solving as well as creative expression.	X	X	X	X	Place out of high-traffic areas—on a grassy knoll or near the transition zone.
Construction materials	Actual tools (child-sized) and small wood pieces for hammering and creating.	Construction materials promote social play, language, and problem solving as well as creative expression.	X	X	X	X	Locate in a supervised area away from other activities. Make sure children wear any necessary protective equipment.
Toy figures and vehicles	Small cars, trucks, trains, dolls, plastic figures, and animals.	Enhance dramatic and role play.	X		X	X	Place in the sandbox or water table or on a table.
Dress-up box	Container of old "outdoorsy" clothes; scarves; fire hats, coats, and hoses; construction helmets and work belts; other dress-up items that children can play in safely while outdoors.	Develops imagination, language, and social play. Develop gross-motor skills and eye-hand coordination.	X		X	X	If feasible, store in or near the playhouse.
Balls	Any object to toss, catch, roll, or kick. All shapes and sizes of balls, bean bags, even paper bags stuffed with newspaper.	Develop gross-motor skills and eye-hand coordination. Encourage interaction with peers and adults through informal or simple organized games.	X	X		X	Rotate balls for variety.
Sidewalk chalk	Biodegradable, nontoxic chalk in a variety of colors, sizes, and shapes.	Helps develop fine-motor skills and creative expression. Also promotes simple group games.	X	X	X	X	Use where chalk will not damage property.
Binoculars or magnifying glass	Objects with lenses.	Allows children to view their outdoor surroundings in a novel way. Independent or adult-supported activity.	X		X	X	Have several available. Make sure they are stored when not in use.

* S = Social   P = Physical   E = Emotional   C = Cognitive

Note: Adapted from *The Universal Playground: A Planning Guide* (pp. 28–32), by Ministry of Education, Province of British Columbia, Special Education and Facilities Branches, 1993, Victoria, B.C., Canada: Author.

Appendix C
Toxic and Nontoxic Vegetation

This list is an attempt to identify the more common toxic and nontoxic vegetation and landscape materials in North America. If you are working in more tropical zones, other plants that could be toxic will exist. Check with a local botanical garden, poison control center, or landscape architect to be sure that you avoid placing toxic plants in the children's play space.

Toxic Garden Plants

Anemone (all species)

Autumn crocus (Colchicum autumnale)

Azalea (Rhododendron, all species)

Bleeding heart (Dicentra)

Bluebell/squill (Scilla nonscripta, peruviana)

Buttercup (Ranunculus, all species)

Calla lily (Zantedeschia aethiopica)

Carnation (Dianthus caryophyllus)

Castor-oil, or castor bean, plant (Ricinus communis)

Chinese or Japanese lantern (Physalis)

Chrysanthemum (Chrysanthemum)

Clematis (Clematis)

Coneflower (Rudbeckia hortensis Bailey)

Daffodil (Narcissus)

Delphinium (Delphinium)

Foxglove (Digitalis purpurea)

Gladiola (Gladiolus)—bulb

Hyacinth (Hyacinthus orientalis)

Iris

Jonquil (Narcissus)

Larkspur (Delphinium, all species)

Lily of the valley (Convallaria)

Lupine (Lupinus, all species)

Morning glory (Ipomoea tricolor)

Narcissus (Narcissus)

Pansy (Viola tricolor)—seeds

Peony (Paeonia officinalis)—root

Primrose (Primula)

Sweet pea (Lathyrus odoratus) (The child would have to eat a very large number of seeds before feeling ill.)

Sweet William (Dianthus barbatus)

Toxic Vegetable Plants

Avocado leaves

Potato (green patches on tubers and above-ground part)

Tomato greens

Rhubarb leaves

Toxic Hedges, Bushes, Trees, and Vines

Beech—all, but particularly European Beech (Fagus, all species, particularly sylvatica)

Box/Boxwood (Buxus sempervirens)

Buckthorn (Rhamnus cathartica)

Burning bush/spindle tree (Euonymous alata)

Caragana

Cherry laurel (Laurocerasus officinalis)

Cherry (Prunus) leaves and twigs

Clematis (Clematis)

Cotoneaster (Cotoneaster)

Daphne (Daphne mezereum)

Elderberry (Sambucus)—not berries

English ivy (Hedera helix)

Holly (Ilex, all species)

Horse chestnut (Aesculus hippocastanum)

Hydrangea—all

Jet bead/jet berry bush (Rhodotypos tetrapetala Makino)

Kentucky coffee tree (Gymnocladus dioica)

Laburnum/goldenchain tree (Laburnum anagyroides)

Lantana (Lantana camara)

Leucothoe (Leucothoe)

Mountain laurel (Kalmia latifolia)

Oak (Quercus, all species)

Oleander (Nerium oleander)

Periwinkle (Vinca minor)

Pieris/lily-of-the-valley bush (Pieris japonica)

Privet (Ligustrum vulgare)

Red mulberry (Morus rubra)

Rhododendron (Rhododendron, all species)

Snowberry/waxberry (Symphoricarpos, all species)

Strawberry bush (Euonymus)

Sumac (Staghorn) (Rhus typhina)

Virginia creeper (Parthenocissus quinquefolia)

Wisteria (Wisteria sinensis)

Yew (Taxus, all species)

Toxic Wild Mushrooms

All mushrooms should be considered toxic until identified by
a mycologist.

Nontoxic Garden Plants

The following plants are considered essentially nontoxic (safe,
not poisonous). Symptoms from eating or handling them are
unlikely, but any plant may cause an unexpected reaction in
certain individuals.

Abelia

Abyssinian sword lily

African daisy

African plum

Airplane plant

Aluminum plant

Aralia

Araucaria

Asparagus fern

Aspidistra (Cast iron plant)

Aster (Callistephus)

Baby's tears

Bachelor buttons

Bamboo

Bird's nest fern

Blood leaf

Boston fern

Bougainvillea

Cactus (certain varieties)

California poppy

Camelia

Coleus species

Corn plant

Crabapple

Creeping Charlie

Creeping Jennie (Moneywort, Lysima)

Croton (house variety)

Dahlia

Daisy

Dandelion

Dogwood

Donkey tail

Dracaena

Easter lily

Echeveria

Eucalyptus

Eugenia

Fuchsia

Forget-me-not (Myosotis)

Gardenia

Geranium (Pelargonium)

Gloxinia (Tinningia speciosa)

Grape ivy

Hedge apple

Hens & Chicks

Hollyhock (Althaea)

Honeysuckle

Hoya

Impatiens

Jade plant

Kalanchoe

Lipstick plant

Magnolia

Marigold

Monkey plant

Mother-in-law tongue

Norfolk Island pine

Peperomia

Phlox

Prayer plant

Purple passion

Pyrocantha

Sanseveria

Scheffelera

Sensitive plant

Snapdragon (Antirrhinum)

Spider plant

Swedish ivy

Umbrella

Violet

Wandering Jew

Weeping fig

Weeping willow

Wild onion

Zebra plant

Nontoxic Hedges and Bushes

False spirea (Astilbe)

Hawthorne/haws (Crataegus)

Honeysuckle (Lonicera, all species)

Lilac (Syringa)

Mock orange (Philadelphus, pittosporum tobira)

Spirea (Spirea japonica)

Remember that any plant in a child's mouth is a foreign object that may obstruct or get into the airway. In a very young child, any plant ingestion may cause mild gastrointestinal upset due to its fiber content.

Note: From *The Early Childhood Playground: An Outdoor Classroom* (pp. 34–35), by S. Esbensen, 1987, Ypsilanti, MI: High/Scope Press; and the Poison Control Center, Children's Hospital of Michigan, Detroit, MI. Used with permission.

Appendix D
Resources

For information on the National Playground Safety Institute's forms as well as general playground information, contact:

National Recreation and Park Association (NRPA)
22377 Belmont Ridge Road
Ashburn, VA 20148
Phone: 703-858-0784
Fax: 703-858-0794
Web site: *www.nrpa.org*
E-mail: *info@nrpa.org*

For a listing of resources regarding playground safety and injury prevention, contact:

National Program for Playground Safety
University of Northern Iowa
School of Health, Physical Education & Leisure Services
Cedar Falls, Iowa 50614-0161
Phone: 800-554-7529
Fax: 319-273-5833
Web site: *www.uni.edu/playground/*
E-mail: *playground-safety@uni.edu*

For specific information on playground equipment and surface standards, contact:

American Society for Testing and Materials (ASTM)
100 Barr Harbor Drive
West Conshohocken, PA 19428-2959
Phone: 610-832-9500
Fax: 610-832-9555
Web site: *www.astm.org*
E-mail: *webmastr@astm.org*

To obtain a copy of the current *Handbook for Public Playground Safety* or to report a product hazard, contact:

U.S. Consumer Product Safety Commission (CPSC)
Washington, DC 20207
Phone: 800-638-2772
Fax: 301-504-0124
Web site: *www.cpsc.gov*
E-mail: *info@cpsc.gov*

For information on articles related to developmentally appropriate practice and playground design, contact:

National Association for the Education of Young Children (NAEYC)
1509 16th Street, NW
Washington, DC 20036
Phone: 800-424-2460
Fax: 202-328-1846
Web site: *www.naeyc.org*
E-mail: *naeyc@naeyc.org*

For information on adult play leadership, children's right-to-play issues, and playground design, contact:

The American Association for the Child's Right to Play
c/o Dr. Rhonda Clements, President
240 Hofstra University
Hempstead, NY 11549
Phone: 516-463-5176
E-mail: *hprrlc@hofstra.edu*

To obtain information on regulations for making playgrounds accessible for individuals with disabilities, contact:

U.S. Access Board
1331 F Street NW, Suite 1000
Washington, DC 20004-1111
Phone: 800-872-2253
Fax: 202-272-5447
Web site: *www.access-board.gov*
E-mail: *info@access-board.gov*

For information on school and community playgrounds and playground accessibility, contact:

American Alliance for Health, Physical Education, Recreation and Dance
1900 Association Drive
Reston, VA 20191
Phone: 800-321-0789 (be sure to ask for AALR)
Web site: *www.aahperd.org*
E-mail: *webmaster@aahperd.org*

To obtain a copy of the current Canadian playground standard, contact:

Canadian Standards Association
Head Office
178 Rexdale Boulevard
Etobicoke, Ont., Canada
M9W 1R3
Phone: 416-747-4000
             800-463-6727 (U.S. and Canada only)
Fax: 416-747-4149
Web site: *www.csa.ca*
E-mail: *certinfo@csa.ca*

The Canadian Parks/Recreation Association sponsors workshops across Canada on making playgrounds conform to the standards set by the Canadian Standards Association.

CP/RA
306-1600 James Naismith Drive
Gloucester, Ont., Canada
K1B 5N4
Phone: 613-748-5651
Fax: 613-748-5854
Web site: *www.activeliving.ca/activeliving/cpra.html*
E-mail: *cpra@activeliving.ca*

The following organization is dedicated to the health and well-being of Canadian children by making available resources on health promotion and disease and injury prevention.

Canadian Institute of Child Health
885 Meadowlands Drive, Ste. 512
Ottawa, Ont., Canada
K2C 3N2
Phone: 613-224-4144
Fax: 613-224-4145
Web site: *www.cich.ca*
E-mail: *cich@igs.net*

Appendix E
Anthropometry of Children 2–8½ Years of Age

Stature

Age	Mean		Minimum		Maximum	
yr	in.	cm	in.	cm	in.	cm
2.0–3.5	36.8	93.4	32.0	81.3	42.7	108.5
3.5–4.5	39.9	101.4	35.8	90.9	44.9	114.1
4.5–5.5	42.6	108.3	38.0	96.5	49.0	124.4
5.5–6.5	45.1	114.6	38.0	96.5	51.7	128.7
6.5–7.5	47.8	121.2	41.9	106.3	52.7	133.8
7.5–8.5	50.0	126.9	43.9	111.5	55.6	140.6

Standing Height From Feet to Armpit

Age	Mean		Minimum		Maximum	
yr	in.	cm	in.	cm	in.	cm
2.0–3.5	25.7	65.2	23.4	59.5	29.0	73.6
3.5–4.5	28.3	72.0	25.4	64.6	32.4	82.2
4.5–5.5	30.8	78.2	26.2	66.6	35.4	89.8
5.5–6.5	33.0	83.8	29.2	74.2	37.2	94.6
6.5–7.5	35.0	88.9	30.2	76.6	40.6	103.0
7.5–8.5	37.0	94.1	33.3	84.6	42.4	107.7

Standing Center of Gravity

Age	Mean		Minimum		Maximum	
yr	in.	cm	in.	cm	in.	cm
2.0–3.5	22.0	56.0	20.2	51.2	24.1	61.2
3.5–4.5	23.4	59.4	21.6	54.9	25.2	64.0
4.5–5.5	25.4	64.5	23.8	60.5	27.2	69.0
5.5–6.5	26.0	66.2	22.2	56.5	28.9	73.4
6.5–7.5	27.6	70.0	25.3	64.3	30.6	77.6
7.5–8.5	28.7	72.8	26.3	66.9	30.9	78.4

Step Height

Age	Mean		Minimum		Maximum	
yr	in.	cm	in.	cm	in.	cm
2.0–3.5	13.1	33.3	8.7	22.1	18.5	47.1
3.5–4.5	15.6	39.6	10.6	26.9	21.9	55.5
4.5–5.5	16.9	42.9	12.1	30.8	22.4	57.0
5.5–6.5	19.8	50.4	13.9	35.4	27.3	69.4
6.5–7.5	20.7	52.6	13.3	33.8	27.2	69.2
7.5–8.5	21.6	54.9	16.0	40.7	29.8	75.7

Head Height

Age	Mean		Minimum		Maximum	
yr	in.	cm	in.	cm	in.	cm
2.0–3.5	6.8	17.3	5.8	14.8	7.8	19.7
3.5–4.5	7.0	17.9	6.4	16.2	8.0	20.4
4.5–5.5	7.0	17.9	6.4	16.4	8.0	20.2
5.5–6.5	7.2	18.4	6.3	15.9	8.3	21.2
6.5–7.5	7.4	18.7	6.3	15.9	8.4	21.4
7.5–8.5	7.4	18.8	6.4	16.2	8.4	21.3

Head Breadth

Age	Mean		Minimum		Maximum	
yr	in.	cm	in.	cm	in.	cm
2.0–3.5	5.3	13.4	4.7	11.9	5.9	15.0
3.5–4.5	5.4	13.7	4.9	12.4	7.0	17.9
4.5–5.5	5.4	13.8	4.9	12.5	6.1	15.6
5.5–6.5	5.5	13.9	5.0	12.7	6.3	15.9
6.5–7.5	5.6	14.1	5.0	12.7	6.2	15.7
7.5–8.5	5.6	14.2	5.2	13.1	6.4	16.2

Distance From Chin to Back of Head

Age	Mean		Minimum		Maximum	
yr	in.	cm	in.	cm	in.	cm
10–12	7.4	18.9	7.0	17.7	8.2	20.9
13–18	7.6	19.3	7.2	18.2	8.1	20.7
19–24	7.8	19.8	7.3	18.6	8.4	21.3
25–30	8.0	20.3	7.4	18.8	9.0	22.8
31–36	8.1	20.5	7.6	19.2	8.6	21.9
37–42	8.2	20.9	7.9	20.0	8.7	22.2
43–48	8.3	21.0	7.7	19.6	8.9	22.5

Note: From research sponsored by the *U.S. Consumer Product Safety Commission.* (See U.S. Consumer Product Safety Commission, 1977, and Schneider, Lehman, Pflug, & Owings, 1986.)

Appendix F
General Maintenance Checklist and Inspection Forms

The following checklist will assist you in determining the condition of your outdoor equipment and environment. To record your observations in more detail, adapt the inspection forms that follow the checklist to fit your particular needs.

Maintenance Checklist

Surfacing

_____The equipment has adequate protective surfacing under and around it, and the surfacing materials have not deteriorated.

_____Loose-fill surfacing materials have no foreign objects or debris.

_____Loose-fill surfacing materials are not compacted and do not have reduced depth in heavy-use areas such as under swings or at slide exits.

_____Hard surfaces are swept regularly.

General Hazards

_____There are no sharp points, corners, or edges on the equipment.

_____There are no missing or damaged protective caps or plugs.

_____There are no hazardous protrusions or projections.

_____There are no potential clothing entanglement hazards, such as open S-hooks or protruding bolts.

_____There are no pinch, crush, and shearing points or exposed moving parts.

_____There are no trip hazards, such as exposed footings on anchoring devices, or rocks, roots, and other environmental obstacles in the play area.

Deterioration of the Equipment

_____The equipment has no rust, rot, cracks, or splinters, especially where it comes in contact with the ground.

_____There are no broken or missing components on the equipment (e.g., handrails, guardrails, protective barriers, steps, or rungs on ladders), and there are no damaged fences, benches, or signs on the playground.

_____All equipment is securely anchored.

Security of Hardware

_____There are no loose fastening devices or worn connections, such as S-hooks.

_____Moving components, such as swing hangers, are not worn.

Drainage

_____The entire play area has satisfactory drainage, especially in heavy-use areas such as under swings and at slide exits.

Leaded Paint

_____If leaded paint has been used on playground equipment, it has not deteriorated as noted by peeling, cracking, chipping, or chalking.

_____There are no areas of visible leaded paint chips or accumulation of lead dust.

General Upkeep of Playgrounds

_____Loose toys and equipment are clean, kept repaired, and stored when not in use.

_____Standing water is replaced frequently.

_____Sand in sandbox is cleaned regularly and replaced occasionally.

_____The entire playground is free from miscellaneous debris or litter such as tree branches, cans, bottles, glass, etc.

Note: From *Handbook for Playground Safety* (p. 32), U.S. Consumer Product Safety Commission, 1997, Washington, DC: Government Printing Office. Adapted with permission.

High–Frequency Inspection Form (Daily or Routine)*

(Numbers on form correspond to instructions on the following pages.)

Site Name/ID Number: _____1_____

Inspector Name: _____2_____ Date: __3__ Start/Finish Times _____4_____

Repairer Name: _____5_____ Date: __6__ Start/Finish Times _____7_____

8 Use the following codes:

1=Okay 2=Needs maintenance 3=Request for repair O=Supervisor notified and work order written X=Corrective action complete

General Inspection Items	Code	Inspection Comments	Repair Comments
9 Vandalism: Damage, graffiti, glass, trash, needles, etc.	22	23	24
10 Loose or missing hardware			
11 Chains (kinked, twisted, broken)			
12 Guardrails/handrails secure			
13 Seats (cut, cracked, missing)			
14 Wood (rotten, cracked, missing)			
15 Remove foreign objects (ropes, chains, wood, etc.)			
16 Sweep walkways, platforms, steps			
17 Footers (concrete) exposed			
18 Standing water			
19 Objects in surfacing materials			
20 Loose surfacing materials (rake level)			
21 Need surfacing material under:			
Swings			
Climbers			
Fire Pole			
Slide			
Others			
Others			
Others			
Others			
Others			

For office use only

25 Reviewed by Assistant Superintendent of Parks_____Date_____

26 Reviewed by Superintendent of Parks and Planning_____Date_____

27 **IMPORTANT**—This information has been prepared to assist the playground owner's attorney in defending potential litigation. *Do not* release to any person except an agency official, designated claim representative, or an investigating police officer.

28 USE BACK OF FORM FOR ADDITIONAL COMMENTS.

29 REPORT ALL VANDALISM TO ASSISTANT SUPERINTENDENT OF PARKS AND/OR YOUR MAINTENANCE SUPERVISOR.

Note: Forms and instructions on pp. 103–115 taken from *Playground Safety Is No Accident,* 2nd Edition, by K. Kutska and K. Hoffman (in press), Ashburn, VA: National Recreation and Park Association. Copyright 1999 by K. Kutska and K. Hoffman. Adapted with permission.

User's Guide for High-Frequency Inspection Form

1. The playground site name or ID number should be clearly printed at the top of each form used.

2. The inspector's name should be clearly printed on each form used.

3. The inspector should correctly date each form used.

4. The inspector should record the start and finish times for the inspection.

5. The person who conducts any follow-up repairs must clearly print their name on the original inspection form.

6. The person who conducts a follow-up repair must date the form on the day repairs are conducted.

7. The repairer should record the start and finish times related to the equipment repair.

8. The inspection codes located near the top of the form should be used by the initial person conducting the high-frequency playground inspection and any person conducting follow-up repairs. These codes should be placed in the Code column, as necessary.

   The first code *(1=OK)* should be used by the initial inspector to indicate that the equipment inspected is in satisfactory condition.

   The second code *(2=Needs maintenance)* should be used by the initial inspector to indicate that some type of maintenance is needed that can be corrected on site. (Examples include raking loose surfacing materials back into use zones, removing litter, or unwrapping a swing that has been wrapped around its top beam.)

   The third code *(3=Request for repair)* should be used by the initial inspector to indicate that additional assistance is needed to complete a repair that does not create an immediate safety concern. (Examples include minor paint chipping, graffiti vandalism, or a loose playground border timber.)

The fourth code *(O=Supervisor notified and work order requested)* should be used to indicate that a repair is needed that cannot be corrected on site or that is a safety concern. The O code should be placed around a 3 code (i.e., code 3 should be circled), and the playground supervisor should be notified immediately if a significant safety concern exists. Examples include broken equipment, missing parts, or if the structural integrity of equipment is in question. Steps should also be taken to secure the equipment from use in certain cases.

The fifth code *(X=Corrective action complete)* should be used to indicate that a repair has been completed by the initial inspector or a follow-up repair person. The X code should be placed directly over the 2, 3, or O codes.

> **NOTE:** The general inspection items denoted by numbers 9–20 are a listing of common playground equipment problems that should be evaluated while conducting a high-frequency inspection. In no way is this a complete listing of all potential problems that could occur on playground equipment. Persons performing high-frequency inspections must be alert to identify other types of hazards that could exist.

9. Any vandalism noted in the playground area, which could include broken equipment, glass, trash, feces, needles, etc., should be evaluated.
10. Briefly inspect all equipment for any loose or missing hardware.
11. Briefly inspect all swing and chain climbers for any kinks, twists, or broken links.
12. Briefly inspect platforms and stairway guardrails to determine if they are secure.
13. Briefly inspect all swings for missing components, cracks, or cuts.
14. Briefly inspect wooden equipment and structures for missing components, rotting, or severe cracking.

15. Briefly inspect for any foreign objects that may be brought into the playground area such as ropes, chains, wood boards, toys. Remove these materials from the site.

16. Briefly inspect all walkways, stairways, platforms, and steps; sweep up any loose surfacing materials or related substances.

17. Briefly inspect all surface-level areas where playground equipment is secured into the ground for any exposed concrete footings that exist.

18. Briefly inspect any areas under playground equipment and in their use zones for any standing water or excessive amounts of moisture.

19. Briefly inspect loose surfacing materials for any foreign objects, such as glass, metal, or toys, located in the surfacing material.

20. Briefly inspect below playground components that experience a "kick out" of loose surfacing materials and rake back the surfacing materials as needed.

21. List all those areas that experience regular surfacing "kick out" such as under swings and at the bottom of slides. Briefly inspect below these playground components that experience a "kick out" of loose surfacing materials and rake or replace loose surfacing materials as needed.

22. The Code column is used by the initial inspector and follow-up repair person to indicate the appropriate code or status of the playground components or area being inspected.

23. Inspection comments should be made to indicate the actual problem noted during the high-frequency inspection. The inspection comments should indicate the specific piece of equipment concerned and briefly explain the potential safety concern and its location. This section must be completed whenever codes 2, 3, or 0 are used.

24. The Repair comments should reflect the actions taken by the inspector or repairer to correct a playground problem. This sec-

tion must be completed whenever codes 2, 3, or O are used by the inspector. These codes that require corrective action should be marked by an X when repaired.

25. This section should be completed by the assistant superintendent of parks or a comparable position. It should be initialed and dated. This person will typically first receive the results of the high-frequency inspections, and be responsible for generating work orders for follow-up repairs. In the event that a serious playground hazard is noted, this person should be radioed or phoned immediately for instructions.

26. This section should be completed by the superintendent of parks and planning or an equivalent position. It should be initialed and dated by the person responsible for the overall playground safety program and returned to the person responsible for follow-up action or permanent filing.

27. This important information is designed to prevent any person in your agency from releasing the high-frequency inspection form(s) to any outside sources without the consent of your agency's attorney.

28. The playground inspector should use the back of the form to describe in depth any hazards or problems noted during the high-frequency inspection. Do not limit your comments to the boxes provided on the front of the form when additional explanation is necessary.

29. All vandalism or other serious playground hazards noted during a high-frequency inspection must be reported immediately to the maintenance supervisor responsible for the playground safety program.

> **NOTE:** This user's guide should be used during initial inspector training and photocopied and carried into the field as a reference guide for the inspector in completing the form.

Low-Frequency Playground Inspections

Low-frequency (periodic) playground inspections should be conducted on a scheduled basis by a trained employee to evaluate the structural integrity and wear concerns of each individual piece of playground equipment at a park site. The scheduling of low-frequency inspections may range from weekly to monthly depending on existing conditions, environmental conditions, age, use factors, etc.

It is best to make a low-frequency inspection form that is customized to each of your individual park sites. To do this you should begin by compiling an itemized list of all playground components that exist at each individual playground site (see page 110).

Itemizing Park/Playground Components

One of the most important steps in the initial development of your low-frequency inspection forms is the complete listing of all play equipment, play components, and site amenities that exist at each park. If this list can be coupled with a site plan of the play area, it can be an invaluable aid to playground safety inspectors in identifying a specific piece of equipment, especially if multiple types of the same exist (i.e., multi slides, swings, etc.). Many times this list has already been completed by the playground equipment manufacturer. If this information is missing from the playground file, a phone call to the equipment manufacturer may produce a copy of this information from their records. A visit to the site should also be done to identify any site components that may have been added or removed.

Developing a Site Plan

Remember the old saying, "A picture is worth a thousand words"? A site plan or black-and-white photographs can reduce the inspection time by clearly identifying each piece of equipment you are inspecting with a number or code. Inspections must be as simple as possible, and these tools will help reduce inspection time while eliminating some human errors and thereby increasing the degree of consistency from one inspector to another. (See p. 111 for a sample site plan.)

If a site plan cannot be re-created, black-and-white photographs can be taken to create a visual reference for each area within the playground. These photographs can be reproduced or photocopied for easy duplication of records.

Manufacturers may sell similar equipment and components using different names, which can confuse safety inspectors. If a site plan is available, it should be compared to the itemized list of play equipment to ensure accuracy. The plan can then be alphabetically or numerically cross-referenced to the itemized list and labeled. The itemized list must be completed before a low-frequency playground inspection form can be developed for each playground site.

Itemized List of Playground Equipment

Site Name/ID Number_____

Inspector Name:_____   Date:_____

Play Area	Play Component	Description of Play Area or Component	Comments

Low-Frequency Site Plan Inspection Method

Once a comprehensive listing of playground components by site is completed, they can be transferred to the low-frequency/periodic playground inspection form (see page 112).

Site plans (see below) should be combined with the low-frequency inspection form or re-created with black-and-white photographs to document the location of park components to be inspected.

A trained low-frequency playground inspector can then systematically inspect each component in the playground for damage, wear, and other safety concerns. It is very important that the inspector have a substantial level of experience in playground repair methods and current playground safety guidelines. Also, manufacturer maintenance instructions should be closely followed to ensure proper repairs.

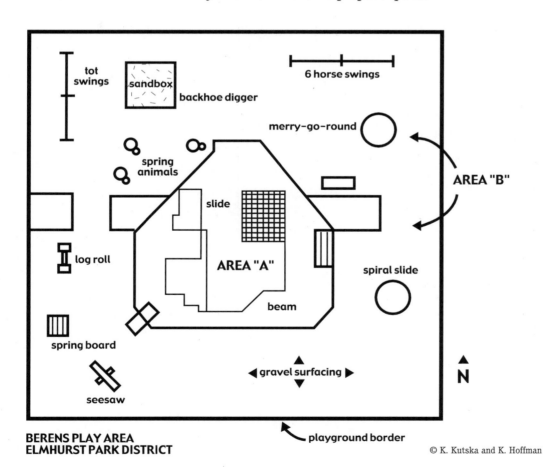

BERENS PLAY AREA
ELMHURST PARK DISTRICT

© K. Kutska and K. Hoffman

Low-Frequency Site Plan Playground Inspection Form

(Numbers on form correspond to instructions on the following pages.)

Site Name/ID Number: _____ *1* _____

Inspector Name: _____ *2* _____   Date: ___ *3* ___   Start/Finish Times _____ *4* _____

Repairer Name: _____ *5* _____   Date: ___ *6* ___   Start/Finish Times _____ *7* _____

8 Use the following codes:

1=Okay 2=Needs maintenance 3=Request for repair O=Supervisor notified and work order written X=Corrective action complete

Area	#	Play Component	Code	Problem (if any)	Action Taken
9	*10*	*11*	*12*	*13*	*14*
15 Playground surfacing material and draining					
16 Playground border/edger (if applicable)					

17 Directions:

1. List each piece of playground equipment in the Play Components column.
2. As each component is inspected, indicate the appropriate codes in the Code column.
3. Describe the nature of any maintenance or follow-up repairs.
4. File each inspection report with your permanent records.

18 Work Order Numbers (list all that apply): _____

19 Supervisor _____ Signature _____ Date _____

20 This form has been prepared to assist the playground owner's attorney in defending potential litigation. *Do not* release to any person except an agency official, designated claim representative, or an investigating officer.

User's Guide for Low-Frequency Site Plan Inspection Form

1. The playground site name or ID number should be clearly printed at the top of each form used.

2. The inspector's name should be clearly printed on each form used.

3. The inspector should correctly date each form used.

4. The inspector should record the start and finish times for the inspection.

5. The person who conducts any follow-up repairs must clearly print their name on the original inspection form.

6. The person who conducts a follow-up repair must date the form on the day repairs are conducted.

7. The repairer should record the start and finish times related to the equipment repair.

8. The first code *(1=Okay)* should be used by the playground inspector to indicate that the equipment inspected is in satisfactory condition.

   The second code *(2=Needs maintenance)* should be used by the inspector to indicate that some form of maintenance is needed and can be corrected on site.

   The third code *(3=Request for repair)* should be used when a maintenance concern has been noted, but repairs cannot be completed while on site and additional follow-up is necessary.

   The fourth code *(O=Supervisor notified and work order written)* should be used to indicate that a serious maintenance or safety consideration exists, and that a supervisor will be notified and a work order completed to correct or minimize the concern. The 3 code should be circled by this code.

   The fifth code *(X=Corrective action completed)* should be used to indicate that a repair has been completed by the inspector or repair person. The X code should be placed directly over the 2, 3, or O codes.

9. The playground components should be grouped into a number of areas on the site plan drawings to assist in identification of each component to be inspected. (If available, indicate the appropriate area number in the first column.)

10. Specific playground components to be inspected should be numbered to assist in their identification.

11. A description of the playground component should be typed or printed.

12. The Code column is used by the initial inspector and follow-up repair person to indicate the appropriate code which relates to the status of the playground components being inspected.

13. The inspector should indicate the nature of a maintenance concern noted during the low-frequency inspection.

14. The inspector or follow-up repair person should indicate what actions were taken to correct a maintenance concern.

15. The low-frequency inspector should evaluate the need for surfacing materials so that adequate levels are available to meet the critical fall height criteria.

16. The inspector should evaluate the condition of any playground borders or edges for maintenance concerns or trip hazards.

17. Four directions are listed to assist the inspector in completing the form.

18. All work orders that are developed to correct a playground maintenance concern should be listed when completed.

19. The playground maintenance supervisor or other manager should print their name and sign and date the form.

20. This important information is designed to prevent any person in your agency from releasing the low-frequency inspection form(s) to any outside sources without the consent of your agency's attorney.

Important Notes on
Low-Frequency Inspections

1. All playground equipment installation and maintenance manuals provided by the manufacturer should be carefully reviewed for any specific maintenance procedures. These specific maintenance procedures should be listed on a separate form and attached to the low-frequency inspection forms.

2. *Specific note:* To protect your agency from voiding any product's liability protection provided through the equipment manufacturer, always closely follow the manufacturer's maintenance instructions and never modify any playground parts in-house without the written permission of the manufacturer.

3. It is recommended that only replacement parts provided by original manufacturers be used in maintaining your playground components. If not, the agency risks voiding the product's liability protection through the manufacturer.

4. In some cases, manufacturers' maintenance checklists are not sufficient for use in a long-term comprehensive playground maintenance program.

Appendix G
Playground Incident Report Form

Name and position of adult completing this report:

Date report completed:

Date and time of incident:

Names, addresses, and birth dates of parties involved (include supervisors present)—
  Students:

  Adults:

Names and addresses of any others who observed the incident:

Describe incident (include exact location):

Source: Theemes, T. (1999). *Let's Go Outside! Designing the Early Childhood Playground.* Ypsilanti, MI: High/Scope Press.

What were the weather conditions at the time of the incident?

Was there any equipment involved in the incident? If so, describe the type of equipment and how it related to the incident.

What is the surfacing on the play area where the incident occurred (include depth)?

Were there any injuries apparent at the time of incident? Describe as accurately as possible.

Describe the actions taken after the incident occurred.

Were parents or guardians notified?

Name(s):

Source: Theemes, T. (1999). *Let's Go Outside! Designing the Early Childhood Playground.* Ypsilanti, MI: High/Scope Press.

Name and position of person who notified parents or guardians:

Describe the outcome of the incident at the time of this report.

Have any precautionary actions been taken at the location?

Include photographs if possible.

Source: Theemes, T. (1999). *Let's Go Outside! Designing the Early Childhood Playground.* Ypsilanti, MI: High/Scope Press.

References

Alberta Recreation and Parks, Recreation and Sport Facilities Section. (1987). *Play space planning.* Edmonton, AB: Author.

American Society for Testing and Materials. (1996). *Standard specification for impact attenuation of surface systems under and around playground equipment* (No. F1292-96). Philadelphia: Author.

American Society for Testing and Materials. (1999). *Standard consumer safety performance specification for playground equipment for public use* (No. F1487-98). Philadelphia: Author.

Ayres, A. J. (1979). *Sensory integration and the child.* Los Angeles, CA: Western Psychological Services.

Ball, D. (1995). Applying risk management concepts to playground safety. In M. L. Christansen (Ed.), *Playground Safety: Proceedings of the 1995 International Conference* (pp. 2–26). University Park: Pennsylvania State University, Center for Hospitality, Tourism and Recreation Research.

Beckwith, J. (1996). *Play value rating scale and universal design guide.* Available from Beckwith and Associates, P.O. Box 1010, Forestville, CA, 95436.

Berk, L. (1997). *Child Development* (4th ed.). Boston: Allyn & Bacon.

Bixler, R. D., Carlisle, C. L., Hammitt, W. E., & Floyd, M. F. (1994). Observed fears and discomforts among urban students on field trips to wildland areas. *Journal of Environmental Education, 26*(1), 24–33.

Blow, S. (1996). Child's play is so clean it's a dirty shame. *Playrights, 18*(4), 4–5.

Bodrova, E. & Leong, D. J. (1996). *Tools of the mind.* Englewood Cliffs, NJ: Prentice Hall.

Boulton, M. J. (1992). Participation in playground activities at middle school. *Educational Research, 34*(3), 167–182.

Esbensen, S. (1987). *The early childhood playground: An outdoor classroom.* Ypsilanti, MI: High/Scope Press.

Frost, J. L. (1996, April). Joe Frost on playing outdoors. *Scholastic Early Childhood Today,* 26–28.

Frost, J. L. (1997, April). Child development and playgrounds. *Parks and Recreation,* 55–60.

Garbarino, J. (1997). Educating children in a socially toxic environment. *Educational Leadership, 54*(7), 12–16.

Goleman, D. (1995). *Emotional intelligence.* New York: Bantam Books.

Greenman, J. (1995, November). Children need to live in the real world. *Child Care Information Exchange,* 58–60.

Guddemi, M., Jambor, T., & Moore, R. (1995). *Advocacy for the child's right to play.* Unpublished manuscript.

Harris, V. (1996). Open-air learning experiences. In N. A. Brickman (Ed.), *Supporting young learners 2: Ideas for child care providers and teachers.* Ypsilanti, MI: High/Scope Press.

Henderson, W. (1997, April). Catching kids: Guidelines to choosing a playground surface. *Parks and Recreation,* 84–92.

Heseltine, P. J. (1995). Safety versus play value. In M. L. Christansen (Ed.), *Playground Safety: Proceedings of the 1995 International Conference* (pp. 109–115). University Park: Pennsylvania State University, Center for Hospitality, Tourism and Recreation Research.

Hohmann, M. & Weikart, D. P. (1995). *Educating young children: Active learning practices for preschool and child care programs.* Ypsilanti, MI: High/Scope Press.

Jensen, M. T. (1995). CEN . . . and the art of motor skill maintenance. In M. L. Christansen (Ed.), *Playground Safety: Proceedings of the 1995 International Conference* (pp. 109–115). University Park: Pennsylvania State University, Center for Hospitality, Tourism and Recreation Research.

Katz, I. G. & McClellan, D. E. (1997). *Fostering children's social competence: The teacher's role.* Washington, DC: National Association for the Education of Young Children.

Kutska, K. & Hoffman, K. (in press). *Playground safety is no accident* (2nd ed.). Ashburn, VA: National Recreation and Park Association.

Landreth, G. L. (1993). Child-centered play therapy. *Elementary School Guidance & Counseling, 28,* 17–29.

Ministry of Education, Special Education and Facilities Branches. (1993). The universal playground: A planning guide. Victoria, B.C., Canada: Author.

Moore, R. C. & Jambor, T. (1995). *Confronting the bogey man: Perceptions and realities of safe neighborhoods for children's play.* Paper presented at the International Association for the Child's Right to Play (USA) conference, Birmingham, AL.

Parten, M. B. (1932). Social participation among preschool children. *Journal of Abnormal and Social Psychology, 27,* 243–269.

Piaget, J. (1952). *The origins of intelligence in children.* New York: Norton.

Richter, J. (1995). Indications to playground planning. In M. L. Christansen (Ed.), *Playground Safety: Proceedings of the 1995 International Conference* (pp. 139–142). University Park: Pennsylvania State University, Center for Hospitality, Tourism and Recreation Research.

Rogers, F. & Sharapan, H. (1993). Play. *Elementary School Guidance & Counseling, 28,* 5–9.

Schneider, L., Lehman, R., Pflug, M., & Owings, C. (1986). *Size and shape of the head and neck from birth to four years* (Final report to the U.S. Consumer Product Safety Commission). Washington, DC: U.S. Government Printing Office.

Supporting young children in resolving conflicts. [Video, 1998]. (Available from High/Scope Press, 600 N. River, Ypsilanti, MI, 48198. 1-800-40-PRESS.)

U.S. Consumer Product Safety Commission (1977). *Anthropometry of infants, children and youths to age 18 for product safety design* (SP-450). Warrendale, PA: Society of Automotive Engineers, Inc.

U.S. Consumer Product Safety Commission (1996). *Tips for public playground safety* (No. 324). Washington, DC: U.S. Government Printing Office.

U.S. Consumer Product Safety Commission (1997). *Handbook for public playground safety* (No. 325). Washington, DC: U.S. Government Printing Office.

Wallach, F. (1997, April). Playground safety update. *Parks and Recreation,* 95–98.

Wassermann, S. (1992). Serious play in the classroom. *Childhood Education, 68*(3), 133–139.

Wilson, R. A., Kilmer, S. J., & Knauerhase, V. (1996, September). Developing an environmental outdoor playspace. *Young Children,* 56–61.

Related Reading

Bredekamp, S. & Copple, C. (Eds.). (1997). *Developmentally appropriate practice in early childhood programs* (Rev. ed.). Washington, DC: National Association for the Education of Young Children.

Bronson, M. B. (1995). *The right stuff for children birth to 8.* Washington, DC: National Association for the Education of Young Children.

Frost, J. L. (1992). *Play and playscapes.* Albany, NY: Delmar.

Greenspan, S. I. (with Salmon, J.). (1993). *Playground politics: Understanding the emotional life of your school-age child.* New York: Addison Wesley.

Harris, V. (1991). The playground: An outdoor setting for learning. In N. A. Brickman & L. S. Taylor (Eds.), *Supporting young learners 1: Ideas for preschool and day care providers.* Ypsilanti, MI: High/Scope Press.

Healy, J. M. (1990). *Endangered minds.* New York: Simon & Schuster.

Moore, R. C. (1993). *Plants for play.* Berkeley, CA: MIG Communications.

Olds, A. R. (1989). Nature as refuge. *Children's Environments Quarterly, 6*(1), 27–32.

Piaget, J. (1962). *Play, dreams and imitation in childhood* (C. Gattegno & F. M. Hodgson, Trans.). New York: Norton.

Roley, S. (1991). Sensory integrative principles and playground design. *Sensory Integration: Special Interest Section Newsletter, 14*(1), 1–6.

Theemes, T. L. (1996, August). *The politics of consequence: A North American perspective.* Paper presented at the International Association for the Child's Right to Play Conference, Espoo, Finland.

Weissbourd, R. (1996). *The vulnerable child.* Reading, MA: Addison Wesley

Index

About the Author

Tracy Theemes is a registered preschool teacher and holds a master's degree in child counseling psychology. Tracy owns and manages KinderMark, a company that designs play areas for lobbies and waiting rooms of commercial businesses.

Prior to starting KinderMark, Tracy worked for an international playground equipment company as manager of sales and marketing and later as head of the research and development department. She represented this company at national regulatory meetings for both the ASTM Public Playground Safety Committee and the Under-2 Playground Safety Committee.

Ms. Theemes has conducted numerous presentations throughout the United States and Canada on topics relating to children and their play environments. Her areas of interest include family marketing concepts, the relationship of children's development to public play-space design, and the influence of the sociocultural context of children on their play.

Tracy resides with her husband, Charles, and their two children, Robert and Elizabeth, in Olympia, Washington.